TRISH

M000030742

iASPIRE

TEEN DEVOTIONS

iAspire to Know God.

iAspire to Serve Others.

iAspire to Be the Best I Can Be.

BARBOUR BOOKS
An Imprint of Barbour Publishing, Inc.

Published by Barbour Books, an imprint of Barbour Publishing, Inc., 1810 Barbour Drive, Uhrichsville, Ohio 44683, www.barbourbooks.com

Our mission is to inspire the world with the life-changing message of the Bible.

 Member of the
Evangelical Christian
Publishers Association

Printed in the United States of America.

To Andrew, Steven, and Jillian:
Aspire to live every day for the glory
of God, and your life will be far
better than anything
you can imagine.

¡ASPIRE TO KNOW GOD.
¡ASPIRE TO SERVE OTHERS.
¡ASPIRE TO BE THE BEST I CAN BE.

You want your life to matter, and this book encourages you to aspire to greatness—God's best for you.

A companion to Barbour's *iAspire Teen Study Bible*, this collection of thought-provoking devotions addresses 101 topics vital to Christian living, with entries such as

- ▶ iAspire to Follow Jesus
- ▶ iAspire to Use My Time Wisely
- ▶ iAspire to Be Kind
- ▶ iAspire to Fight Selfishness
- ▶ iAspire to Finish Well

Written especially for teens, these devotions offer you biblical guidance for wise living. And each entry concludes with a section called "iAspire to Know More," offering additional scriptures or questions for further consideration.

You aspire to great things. Read on to see how God's Word gets you there!

NOTE: Most of the scriptures quoted in this *iAspire* devotional are taken from the New Life Bible, a version originally created for missions. Though it often reads differently than more common translations, we hope you find its unique way of explaining theological ideas helpful. Of course, you're welcome (and encouraged!) to look up the verses in other Bible versions too.

¡ASPIRE TO KNOW GOD

*"This is life that lasts forever. It is to know You,
the only true God, and to know Jesus
Christ Whom You have sent."*

JOHN 17:3

There are two kinds of people in the world: those who know God and those who don't.

Does it seem overly simple to put *everybody* into one of two categories? There are more than seven billion people on our planet—and every person is totally unique.

But without a doubt, what matters most is whether or not we know God.

In fact, what you believe about God is the most important detail about you. It's more important than how you look or who you know or what you own.

In light of eternity, none of those things matter.

What matters is who you trust with your eternity.

The most well-known verse in the whole Bible is John 3:16:

*"For God so loved the world that He gave His
only Son. Whoever puts his trust in God's Son will
not be lost but will have life that lasts forever."*

God's Son is Jesus, who is God in human flesh. It's okay if that's hard to understand. People have wrestled with the idea of the Trinity—one God in three "persons" (Father, Son, and Holy Spirit)—for millennia. But even if He's hard to understand, God is 100 percent real.

And God is the most important person who has ever existed. He's all-powerful and He knows everything. He brought the world into existence with a single word, and He keeps everything going by His will. He knows every detail about your past and your future. And He promises that in the end, He'll remake this world and destroy those who oppose Him.

The best news you will hear today is that this same all-knowing, all-powerful God wants to know *you*. And He's gone to great lengths to make it possible for you to know *Him*.

So whether you know God is the most important fact about you.

He made you. He loves you. He has your best in mind.

God's Son, Jesus Christ, came into the world to rescue you from God's wrath over sin—to make it possible for you to have a personal relationship with God both now and forever.

So the most important thing about you is not *you*. The most profound thing about you is that the God of this universe cares for you—and even more than that, He delights in you. And He wants you to delight in Him.

He invites you to seek Him every day through prayer and Bible reading. In fact, you will never regret a single minute you spend getting to know God.

Today and for the rest of eternity, knowing God makes all the difference.

¡ASPIRE TO KNOW MORE

- ▶ Read 1 Corinthians 8:3 to find a major clue for how we can know God. How does this change your understanding of what it takes to know Him?

- ▶ Look up Ephesians 1:4. If you have placed your faith and trust in Christ, how long does this verse say that God has known you?

- ▶ Ask God to help you know Him better. He wants you to know Him, and He'll help you achieve that goal.

¡ASPIRE TO FOLLOW JESUS

*Jesus said to His followers, "If anyone wants to
be My follower, he must forget about himself.
He must take up his cross and follow Me."*

MATTHEW 16:24

Your decision to follow Jesus today—as a teenager—will shape your entire future. That's exciting, isn't it? You don't have to wait to follow Jesus!

So what does following Jesus actually look like?

The first way we follow Jesus is by repenting of—turning away from—our sin and believing in Jesus for our salvation. Romans 10:9 says,

*If you say with your mouth that Jesus is Lord, and believe
in your heart that God raised Him from the dead,
you will be saved from the punishment of sin.*

The second way we follow Jesus is by imitating His example—and we see that as we read the Bible. We learn to hate the things God hates and love the things He loves.

This process is called *sanctification*, and it's a work God does within us as we follow Jesus. You see, many people in this world are good at *saying* they believe in God, but the choices they make don't back up their claim.

To truly follow Jesus means we seek to please Him in everything we do. We'll never do that perfectly—because we're human—but we'll live genuinely and consistently, even when it's hard.

Sanctification is a lifelong process that ends in *glorification*—seeing God face to face in heaven. The journey between sanctification and glorification is a wonderful path where we learn to know and love the Lord.

Here's some good news: if you want to follow Jesus, He'll help you do that. He never commands us to do anything without also giving us the courage and the ability to obey.

It doesn't matter whether you've grown up hearing the Bible and knowing about Jesus or if this is all brand-new to you. Following Jesus is a decision you have to make for yourself, and if you want to, *you can choose to do it today*. He'll help you!

If you're waiting until you're older to "get serious about God," you're missing a major opportunity right now to know and serve Him. And you're assuming you'll have the time in which to make that happen. But nobody is promised tomorrow.

The wisest thing you can do today—and every day—is aspire to follow Jesus.

¡ASPIRE TO KNOW MORE

▶ Find Matthew 10:22. How did Jesus describe the life of following Him? What makes following Jesus worthwhile?

▶ The decision to follow Jesus requires us to do more than pray a prayer and then live however we want to live. Look up 1 John 2:3-6. What does God say about someone who claims to be a child of God but doesn't live like it?

▶ Does Jesus understand how hard it is to be a Christian? Read John 15:18.

iASPIRE TO WORSHIP THE LORD

Give to the Lord the honor that belongs to Him.
Worship the Lord in the beauty of holy living.
PSALM 29:2

Worship of God is one of the most authentic evidences that we belong to Him.

Many people say they know God. Many people even go to church and put money in the offering. But far fewer people actually worship God with their lives.

So, what does it mean to *worship the Lord*?

Worship is far bigger than the music we sing at church. Certainly, worship can include music if we're truly singing to God, but that's only a part of the picture. Worship is actually showing somebody's worth in a wholehearted way.

Think about the most committed sports fan you know. Chances are, he or she does more than simply watch a game once in a while or mention the team in casual conversation.

No, this person probably wears team gear, talks endlessly about how great the team is, and still loves the team even during its worst seasons. The most committed sports fans go so far as to paint their faces (even their bodies!) on game day. When the camera pans the crowd during a game, you can easily spot the most zealous fans.

This type of dedication can be a form of worship. A true worshiper adores the object of his or her worship more than anything else. Unfortunately, people often worship people and things instead of God, the only being truly worthy of worship.

Why worship the Lord? First, because *He requires it*. The Ten Commandments begin by saying,

"Have no gods other than Me."

EXODUS 20:3

Second, we worship God because *He deserves it*. Revelation 4:11 says, "Our Lord and our God, it is right for You to have the shining-greatness and the honor and the power. You made all things. They were made and have life because You wanted it that way."

God deserves our absolute, wholehearted worship.

So compare your love for God to the love of a passionate sports fan. Our love for Him should be infinitely bigger and better. But when we worship God, it isn't just a duty—it's a delight.

We don't need team gear or face paint to demonstrate our commitment to God. But our love for Him shouldn't be a secret either. People in our lives shouldn't be surprised to learn that we belong to God. Let's talk about Him and make sure everyone around us is invited to know and love Him too.

When it comes to our worship, there is no neutral ground. We're either worshiping the God who created us or we're worshiping something else.

Let's aspire to give our worship and honor to God alone. . .and to delight in doing it.

¡ASPIRE TO KNOW MORE

- ▶ Find John 4:23-24 to see what kind of worship God requires.

- ▶ In what ways should our commitment to Christ look like a sports fan's commitment to a team? In what ways should it look different?

- ▶ We worship God because His worth is infinite. Look up the word *infinite* to see what it means.

¡ASPIRE TO GIVE THANKS

*In everything give thanks. This is what God
wants you to do because of Christ Jesus.*

1 THESSALONIANS 5:18

We always have something to be grateful for.

But sometimes that truth can be hard to believe.

When things aren't going well in our lives, it's tough to see what is good. Very often, our difficult or disappointing experiences fill our minds with complaints, crowding out any thoughts of the gifts God has given. And sometimes—if we're really honest—we may think we don't actually have that much to be thankful for. . .certainly not compared to other people who have *more*.

Question: Do you have a lot of money?

You may be thinking, "Nope."

Very few people actually think they have a lot of money.

But did you know that more than 700 million people around the world live on less than two dollars a day? That's not because they're cheap—that's all they have. In other words, for millions and millions of people, $1.90 is all they have to pay for food, clothing, transportation, a place to live, and any other personal needs.

Many people live in *poverty*—which is just another way of saying *they have very little*.

If you spend more than $1.90 today—or if someone spends more than $1.90 on you—you are far richer than much of the world. And your bad day is probably better than the *best day* of a lot of people.

It's easy—and common—to be ungrateful. But that doesn't mean it's good. When we're unhappy with our stuff, we don't need a change of circumstances as much as we need a change of perspective.

If you have your physical needs met, you have *much* to be thankful for.

Jesus gave us the ultimate example of this in Luke 22. On the same night He would be betrayed—ultimately leading to His painful, undeserved death on a cross—Jesus hosted a supper for His disciples. First, He took a cup and gave thanks for the wine that symbolized His own blood that would soon be shed. Then, He took bread and gave thanks before breaking it into pieces and saying,

> *"This is My body which is given for you.*
> *Do this to remember Me."*
> LUKE 22:19

Jesus—who knew the horrible events that were about to happen in His life—still thanked God for what He had been given.

And we should do the same—even when life doesn't feel good.

There is always, *always* something to be grateful for.

¡ASPIRE TO KNOW MORE

▶ Think of one thing you've never thanked God for, and make it right. Say thanks!

▶ Read 1 Chronicles 16:34. Why should we give thanks to the Lord?

▶ Find 2 Timothy 3:1-5, which describes how people will live in the last days. Look at verse 2. What is linked to not being holy?

¡ASPIRE TO LOVE THE CHURCH

There are many people who belong to Christ.
And yet, we are one body which is Christ's. We are
all different but we depend on each other.

ROMANS 12:5

If you think living the Christian life is hard, *you're right.*

But guess what? You don't need to live this life on your own!

It was not God's design—and it has never been His desire—for us to live in isolation. As human beings, we were created to live, serve, and worship together.

In fact, the only part of creation that God did not describe as "good" was the solitary Adam. God actually said,

> *"It is not good for man to be alone. I will*
> *make a helper that is right for him."*

GENESIS 2:18

God created Eve so that Adam wouldn't be left by himself.

Since that time, it has always been God's good plan for His people to help each other.

One of God's greatest gifts—after our salvation—is the church.

God designed the church as a place for believers to worship Him and help each other on our journey to heaven. He could have commanded that we simply read our Bibles and obey His commands on our own—and it would have been His right to do whatever He pleased. But God graciously gave us the church for His glory and for our good.

Strangely enough, the church is made up entirely of sinful people. True Christians are forgiven for their sins but still struggle to live perfectly. And sometimes, we struggling Christians do and say things that hurt others.

It's just what we do. Every single one of us sins.

The sinful choices of our fellow Christians can be confusing, leaving us with many questions. But they should never be a reason to turn our backs on the good gift God has given us—the church. He handpicked the people He wanted to be part of your life and put them in the church you attend so that you will grow to be more like Jesus.

When you love His people, you are showing love for God.

So what does it look like to love the church?

The three greatest things you can do for your church are *be faithful* to it, *serve* it, and *pray often* for it. In fact, if you start doing these things right now, you'll have as much impact as the oldest, wisest member of your church family.

That's one awesome fact about the church: *you* are just as needed and valuable as any member of the congregation. You don't need to be any older than you are now to love and serve your church.

In fact, God wants you to start right now.

¡ASPIRE TO KNOW MORE

▶ Find Ephesians 5:25. Jesus loved the church enough that He gave what for her?

▶ Look up Matthew 18:20. When we meet as a church family, who meets with us?

▶ You have everything you need to impact your church for the glory of God. Which of the three things—*faithfulness, service, prayer*—can you start doing this week?

iASPIRE TO DO WHAT'S RIGHT

If you know what is right to do but
you do not do it, you sin.
JAMES 4:17

We don't earn God's approval by doing good works.

The truth is, God couldn't love you any more right now than He already does. His love for you is infinite and eternal.

So why is it so important to do what's right?

Very simply, because *we love God*, and we show Him that we love Him by doing what He tells us in His Word.

Hours before the most important event in history—when Jesus would die on the cross—He said these words to His disciples:

"If you love Me, you will do what I say."
JOHN 14:15

Jesus didn't instruct His disciples to keep His commandments so that they could get into heaven or even so that they would be a good example. He didn't promise them that He would fill their lives with blessings and rewards if they did good deeds. Jesus simply told them that obeying Him was proof that they loved Him.

The same is true for us today. If we love God, we'll obey Him.

But let's be honest—sometimes doing what's right can be complicated.

As you get older, you'll meet more and more people with strong opinions about what's right and what's wrong. Oftentimes, these strong opinions clash. Some people may tell you, for example, that the most important thing is your *happiness*. Other people—those in your church, probably—will tell you the most important thing is your *holiness*.

And sometimes even people at church have conflicting opinions about what's right and wrong. There will be times when we do what's right and upset people who think we should have done something else.

So what do we do? How do we know the right thing to do or believe?

For the child of God, it's as simple—and as challenging—as reading our Bibles carefully to find out what God says is right and wrong. The standard for righteousness is not the opinions of others—it's the character of God.

What does God truly say in His Word?

You get to discover that as you spend time with Him reading the Bible.

Here's an important point: talking about doing right will always be easier than actually doing right—but your faith is only as real as your willingness to obey what God commands.

So find out what He says in His Word *and then do it*.

¡ASPIRE TO KNOW MORE

▶ Does God save us because of our good works? If not, why? Find Titus 3:5 for the answer.

▶ Read 1 Peter 3:14. How does the Bible say you will feel if you suffer for doing what is right? Is this something to be afraid of?

▶ Consider this question: Whose opinion truly matters the most to you? (Hint: pay close attention to whose approval you care most about.)

¡ASPIRE TO BE SINCERE

My children, let us not love with words or in
talk only. Let us love by what we do and in truth.

1 JOHN 3:18

Have you ever spent time thinking about who you truly are?

Maybe you've decided there are actually multiple versions of you. For example:

▶ There's the version of you that your family knows.
▶ There's the version of you that your friends know.
▶ There's the version of you that you know.
▶ There's the version of you that God knows.

While, on one hand, this is normal—we tend to act in different ways depending on our comfort level with people and situations—it may also point to a problem called *insincerity*.

Sincerity is an Old English word that some believe arose from Latin roots meaning "without wax."

Many centuries ago, supposedly, dishonest merchants would fill the cracks in broken pottery with wax then sell the items to unsuspecting shoppers. People would pay good money for what they thought was brand-new pottery only to get home and realize it was broken. . .and useless.

Human beings are masterful at making ourselves look like we aren't broken, without weaknesses or flaws. But the goal for Christians should be to present the same version of ourselves to others that we truly are before the Lord.

This doesn't mean that we pour out our deepest thoughts to everyone in the same way we would tell them to God. Nor does it mean we publicly share every problem we have. It does mean that we try to be the same version of ourselves no matter who we're talking to or what we're doing. We should never pretend to be someone we're not.

Jesus was always the same person, whether He was with a large crowd, or with His disciples, or one-on-one. He was the same person with the woman at the well (who was known for her sin) as He was with John the Baptist (who was known for loving God).

We should seek to follow Jesus' example.

Are you embarrassed to think that your school friends know you love God? Would you be ashamed if your family knew the language you use or the things you laugh about with your friends?

If so, these are signs of insincerity. You should ask God to improve your integrity.

Sincerity shows that we know and love Jesus enough to please Him with our decisions, no matter who is watching. Let's ask God to help us choose sincerity.

¡ASPIRE TO KNOW MORE

▶ Find Romans 12:9. Our love should always be sincere. According to this verse, what are two things we should do to help make that happen?

▶ Read Mark 7:6. Here Isaiah described insincere people. Some honor God with their lips, but what does this verse say about their hearts?

▶ Is there a friend in your life with whom you act differently than you do with other people? If so, pray and ask God for strength to be sincere.

¡ASPIRE TO FIGHT ENVY

A heart at peace gives life to the body,
but envy rots the bones.
PROVERBS 14:30 NIV

We live in a culture of comparison.

You're usually aware of the good things happening to other people, aren't you? And most all of us compare what *we* have to what *others* have. Social media makes this easier than ever. In a matter of seconds, you can scroll through your list of friends to see the cool things everyone else got to buy or to do that you've never had or done.

Honestly, it doesn't usually feel good. Too often, our first response isn't to be happy for our friends but to feel sorry for ourselves.

When our comparison turns to frustration, the Bible calls it envy. And envy has the power to destroy you.

Other sins—though they all grieve God—at least promise us brief moments of pleasure. We might like using something we stole, for example, or enjoy a few minutes of gossiping about someone we don't like. We may be happy to get out of trouble because of the lie we told or take satisfaction in saying something unkind to a person who hurt us.

But when it comes to envy, *there is literally nothing enjoyable about it*.

There is no spike of pleasure, no brief moment of satisfaction. Envy looks and feels bad from the minute you give in.

Envy does its best work by getting you to believe you're missing out on something good. We see the gifts God has given our friends—whether that's talent, intelligence, good looks, fun personalities, popularity, money, relationships, status—and we think we are somehow being overlooked. Or maybe that we are somehow unworthy or unloved.

In reality, God has given you every good thing you need. If you don't have something you want, you can safely assume it's because God alone knows what you need and don't need. And you can be sure He's given you other good gifts to enjoy. The apostle Paul said it best when he wrote,

> *I urge you to live a life worthy of*
> *the calling you have received.*
> EPHESIANS 4:1 NIV

God has made you in such a way that you *will* miss out—and those around you will miss out—if you try to live anybody's life but your own.

Aspire to fully enjoy the good gifts God has given you (and the gifts He's given to others) without falling into the trap of comparison and envy.

---

iASPIRE TO KNOW MORE

▶ We know from 1 Corinthians 12 that God has given every one of His children at least one good gift to use in this life. What talents or abilities has God given you? Have you ever overlooked them because you wished you had other gifts?

▶ Find 1 Corinthians 13:4. Is it possible to be jealous of someone and love that person at the same time?

▶ Today, when you're tempted to envy what someone else has, stop and thank God for blessing that person. Thank Him too for the gifts He has given you.

¡ASPIRE TO KNOW MY IDENTITY

*But you are a chosen people, a royal priesthood, a holy nation,
God's special possession, that you may declare the praises of
him who called you out of darkness into his wonderful light.*

1 PETER 2:9 NIV

Who are you?

Do you ever think about your identity? Do you ever ask yourself questions about who you are or why God put you into your family? Ever wondered if God made a mistake or overlooked some detail of your story?

Asking questions about ourselves is a natural part of growing up. But know this: the enemy of God would love nothing more than for you to believe the wrong answers. In fact, Satan is fully committed to messing up your view of who you are—because if you misunderstand *your* identity, chances are you'll misunderstand God's identity. And that can be a deadly mistake.

Thankfully, we have the Bible to help us find the right answers. Here's the first question to ask: *Who does God say that you are?*

God, the creator of the universe, made you in His own image. He knows how many hairs are on your head and how many days you will walk this earth. In fact, He knew all of this—He knew *you*—before He laid the foundation of the world.

Psalm 139:13–14 says all of us were fearfully and wonderfully made, knit together perfectly in our mothers' wombs. God had a plan for your life from the very beginning!

And even when you chose to sin—as we all do—God pursued you with His unfailing love. In fact, He sent His beloved, only Son to die for your sins. If you are trusting Jesus for your salvation, God's plans for you are only and always good.

If that's not enough, God has a good plan for your future. He is working, right now, to set those plans in motion. And He has promised to complete the work He started in you (Philippians 1:6).

Some of the greatest news in the Bible is found in Romans 8:38-39:

For I know that nothing can keep us from the love of God.
Death cannot! Life cannot! Angels cannot! Leaders cannot!
Any other power cannot! Hard things now or in the future
cannot! The world above or the world below cannot! Any other
living thing cannot keep us away from the love of God
which is ours through Christ Jesus our Lord.

Isn't that awesome? You were made and you are loved by God. *That* is your identity. It doesn't matter what anyone else thinks about you. What matters is what God thinks—and He says He loves you with an everlasting love.

¡ASPIRE TO KNOW MORE

▶ Is there any specific detail about your life that you need to trust God with? If so, talk to Him about it today, knowing *He loves you.*

▶ Read John 1:12. If you put your trust in God, what does He give you the right and power to become?

▶ Find each of these verses: Psalm 103:11, 103:17, 147:11. How do we earn God's favor?

¡ASPIRE TO LIVE WITH PURPOSE

*O man, He has told you what is good. What does the Lord
ask of you but to do what is fair and to love kindness,
and to walk without pride with your God?*

MICAH 6:8

What is your purpose in life?

Maybe you think you're too young to know at this point. Or maybe you already have a dream job in mind or a goal you hope to accomplish in ten or fifteen years.

Either way, why not stop to consider the reason God put you on this earth?

You may not know yet what your job will be or where you'll live or what you'll do with your future—and that is absolutely fine—but you can still know with certainty your life's purpose. Goals and dreams may change over time, but the purpose for your life doesn't.

In fact, your purpose doesn't depend at all on your occupation, your bank account, or your relationship status. What *is* your purpose? Simply this: God has called you to live for His glory right where you are.

*So if you eat or drink or whatever you do,
do everything to honor God.*

1 CORINTHIANS 10:31

Long before Jesus was speaking to large crowds or performing miracles or teaching His disciples, He was a boy working alongside His earthly father, Joseph the carpenter. Other than one story of Jesus as a twelve-year-old, there are almost thirty years of Jesus' life that scripture says nothing about—not because those years weren't important or necessary, but because Jesus was simply serving God in the daily responsibilities He'd been given. He was glorifying God in His education and with His family. He was honoring God in His chores and in His relationships.

And the same should be true for you.

Whether you're taking a math class or working a minimum wage job or learning to drive a car, your purpose in life is *to obey and glorify God.*

We may be tempted to think our identity depends on the people we know or the money we make. We may worry about what our friends and acquaintances think of us (though it's likely they're not thinking of us much at all, since they're worried about the same stuff in their lives that we worry about in ours). Yes, that's an aside, but an important one. Now back to the real point: God wants us to live for *Him* no matter what else we're doing.

While it certainly matters what you choose to do with your career and life goals, you should know that—from God's perspective—those things aren't your purpose. They aren't your identity. The identity that matters to God is whether or not you belong to Him.

Anything less than God's glory is too low a purpose for living.

¡ASPIRE TO KNOW MORE

▶ Find Ecclesiastes 12:13. What are the two things every person must do?

▶ Read Ephesians 2:10. According to this verse, God wants you to work for whom?

▶ Which do you think matters most—building *careers* or building *character*? Why?

¡ASPIRE TO SEEK GOD'S APPROVAL

*Do you think I am trying to get the favor of men,
or of God? If I were still trying to please men,
I would not be a servant owned by Christ.*

GALATIANS 1:10

Whether we realize it or want to admit it, every one of us is starving for approval.

We don't all seek approval from the same people or groups. But whether the approval we want is from a pastor or a peer, a date or a dad, we're all wired to look outside ourselves for acceptance and appreciation.

Sometimes we hope people will see and approve a version of ourselves that we present publicly, not the actual version of who we truly are.

Social media makes this really obvious. People will do nearly anything to earn the likes, follows, and shares of other people—even people they've never met. Every day, people risk their lives making videos that they hope will go viral just to earn the approval of strangers watching on the Internet.

Nowhere in the Bible does God forbid us from seeking approval—but He does say the only person we should turn to is *Him*. That's a kind and gracious thing because God sees and loves you for who you really are.

He made you! He knows you! He loves you!

Earning and keeping human approval is very difficult. People are fickle—they change quickly and show very little true loyalty or love. And it can be devastating to put all our effort into earning people's approval only to have that approval yanked away.

God's approval, on the other hand, isn't unpredictable. In fact, in the Old Testament, God spoke to Israel through His servant Malachi saying, "I, the Lord, do not change" (Malachi 3:6).

In the New Testament, Jesus described how His Father watches over people, approving and blessing those who honor Him. Three times in Matthew 6, Jesus said, "Your Father Who sees in secret will reward you" (vv. 4, 6, 18). But Jesus also warned,

> *"Be sure you do not do good things in front of others*
> *just to be seen by them. If you do, you have*
> *no reward from your Father in heaven."*
>
> MATTHEW 6:1

We can do bad things with bad motives, but Jesus says we can also do good things with bad motives! The only time we're doing good things with good motives is when we're doing them for God and His glory.

You don't need to be the funniest, best-looking, or smartest person to earn God's approval. All you need to do is obey His Word and trust Him with the details of your life.

When we're seeking only God's approval, our addiction to human "likes" and "follows" suddenly starts to weaken. We find the freedom that is offered exclusively in Christ.

God's approval is the only approval you need today—and every day.

¡ASPIRE TO KNOW MORE

▶ Be honest with yourself. Whose approval matters most to you right now? If it isn't God's, stop and ask Him to help you in this area.

▶ Find Matthew 5:16. When we do good deeds, who should get the credit?

¡ASPIRE TO USE MY GIFTS

*God has given each of you a gift. Use it to help
each other. This will show God's loving-favor.*

1 PETER 4:10

God has uniquely gifted you with certain talents and abilities, and He wants you to use them.

Maybe you're good at music or teaching children. Maybe you excel at making people feel welcome. Maybe you're talented in the kitchen and like preparing food for people in need. Maybe you can help with the audiovisuals at church, or maybe you're good at something not included on this list.

If you don't know what your gift from God is, keep looking. He's given particular talents and abilities to every one of His children.

There are hundreds of ways that we—as children of God—can minister to others, and God wants us to use our gifts in service to Him.

Did you know that God gives you good gifts specifically so you can serve others? He didn't give you talents to make you prideful or to advance your own agenda. He gave you gifts for the good of others. And now He wants you to serve His people.

Way back in the Bible, Abraham was a man who was greatly blessed by God. In Genesis 12, God promised to give Abraham children, fame, and honor. But God didn't do those thing so Abraham could build a big following or feel good about himself and his popularity.

No. As He finished making His promise to Abraham, God said,

> *"Good will come to all the families
> of the earth because of you."*

GENESIS 12:3

All of the good things God gave Abraham were meant to bless God's people. *God blesses us to bless others!*

Church was never meant to be a spectator sport. Nobody's role should be sitting back and watching others serve—or worse, sitting back and waiting to be served.

It doesn't matter how young you are. You are uniquely qualified to serve God in your church in some way. Now, your job is to figure out—with God's help—where you belong and how you can contribute. What gifts has God given you? What can you do to help others?

Two of Satan's greatest lies that distract people from using their gifts for God's glory are (1) you don't have gifts worth using, and (2) people around you have better gifts or talents than you have.

Neither of these is true.

God has given you some gift to use for the good of others. *So do it.*

¡ASPIRE TO KNOW MORE

▶ Contact your pastor or someone in church leadership and ask what needs your church family has. Consider their answers, and pray about what God would want you to do next.

▶ Read 1 Corinthians 12:4-7. Why does the Holy Spirit work in each person?

▶ Look up Romans 12:4-8. How should you respond to the gift(s) God has given you?

¡ASPIRE TO DO MY BEST

Do not work hard only when your owner sees you.
You would be doing this just to please men.
Work as you would work for Christ. Do what
God wants you to do with all your heart.

EPHESIANS 6:6

None of us will be perfect in this life.

Paul, the New Testament writer, understood this when he wrote,

I do not say that I have. . .already become perfect.
But I keep going on to make that life my own
as Christ Jesus made me His own.

PHILIPPIANS 3:12

Paul knew he wouldn't live a perfect life, but he determined to do his best for Jesus Christ. So should we.

Your assignment in life *right now* is whatever God has given you to do *right now*. And the best way to respond is by doing your best to please Him in every area.

In Genesis 39 we read about Joseph, who endured betrayal from his brothers, separation from his father, and an accusation from his boss's wife. He eventually became the second most powerful man in Egypt—but only after spending twelve years as a slave or prisoner.

Joseph knew both the privilege of power and the pain of prison. And in each case he did his best to please the Lord.

Sometimes schoolwork, sports practice, music lessons, or church activities don't feel like a calling. Maybe we'd rather serve God in an exotic place or with a significant job or alongside a special person. But the training ground for what God might call you to do in the future is how you respond to His assignments *today*. As the apostle Paul put it,

Everyone should live the life the Lord gave to him.
1 CORINTHIANS 7:17

Are you doing your best, or are you satisfied with slopping through your assignments? Do you believe you can please God now, or are you waiting for some "better" assignment before you commit to doing your best?

Don't wait for an important job to do—you have an important job to do right now. Your job is to please the Lord right where He's put you.

Don't wish away this season of life hoping for something better—you'll miss out on what He's created you to do now.

Aspire to do your best *right where you are*.

¡ASPIRE TO KNOW MORE

▶ Do you have a job or responsibility you don't enjoy? How can you do your best to please the Lord despite how you feel?

▶ Read Genesis 39:21-23. Who was with Joseph and showed him kindness when times were hard?

¡ASPIRE TO BE A LEADER

*"For the Son of Man came not to be cared for. He came to care
for others. He came to give His life so that many could be bought
by His blood and made free from the punishment of sin."*
MATTHEW 20:28

Aspiring to leadership is a good thing.

Leadership is simply taking steps to move a person—or a group of people—toward a specific goal. In the world of business, that may mean moving people toward a sales objective. In education, that could mean moving students toward a certain SAT score. In the Christian life, it should mean moving a person—or group of people—toward Christlikeness.

Every Christian should want to be a leader. And here's the key measure of success: Do the people in your life look more or less like Jesus after spending time with you?

It doesn't matter whether you believe you have the right personality or talents to lead. All through the Bible, God delighted in choosing the least likely men and women to lead on His behalf. God called a shepherd boy to be king of Israel. He guided a prostitute to shelter the spies who would overthrow Jericho—then included that woman in the family line of Jesus. God converted a persecutor of Christians then used him to spread the Gospel and write many books in the New Testament.

The list of unlikely leaders is long.

Today, if you feel unlikely, you may be the perfect candidate to serve God—because you're more ready to rely on *His* strength, less on your own.

Unlikely leaders all have something in common, and if you want to lead, you'll need it too: an understanding that true leadership ultimately requires sacrifice.

Christian leadership isn't about being seen as important. It's about being a servant.

Jesus set the ultimate example:

Jesus has always been as God is. But He did not hold to His rights as God. He put aside everything that belonged to Him and made Himself the same as a servant who is owned by someone. He became human by being born as a man. After He became a man, He gave up His important place and obeyed by dying on a cross.

PHILIPPIANS 2:6–8

One clear mark of a leader is that he or she makes the good of other people a guiding principle in every decision. Good leadership isn't based on what feels good or comfortable. But it always solves problems and serves others.

Ready to step up and lead? God is ready to give you wisdom and courage.

¡ASPIRE TO KNOW MORE

▶ Read 1 Corinthians 1:20–25 to discover why God uses unlikely leaders.

▶ Has God used any unlikely people in your life to draw you closer to Him? If so, whom?

▶ Pray and ask God for the chance to be a leader in your school, home, or church.

¡ASPIRE TO PLEASE THE LORD

Learn how to please the Lord.
EPHESIANS 5:10

Learning to please God is something His followers have been doing for thousands of years.

And for centuries, good Christian people have disagreed on which laws or rules to follow in order to earn God's favor. Laws and rules, after all, are nothing new.

The first five books of your Bible—from Genesis to Deuteronomy—are often called "the books of the law." These books record the rules that God gave the children of Israel way back when. Over *six hundred* commands taught them about His character.

Can you imagine trying to keep six hundred rules?

If you're thinking it would be impossible, you're right. Old Testament laws exist, in part, to show us that we're imperfect and need a Savior.

Thankfully, as Christians, we don't need to follow all six hundred-plus Old Testament laws. But we should still care very much about learning God's character and how to please Him. The Old Testament isn't in your Bible by mistake.

So how do we please God? In the New Testament, the apostle Paul wrote,

> *Do as God would do. Much-loved children*
> *want to do as their fathers do.*
> EPHESIANS 5:1

Later in that same chapter, Paul said, "Learn how to please the Lord" (v. 10).

We can draw at least two conclusions from this command: First, it's possible to please the Lord or we wouldn't have been told to do it. In fact, God's given us an entire Bible full of specific ways we can please Him. He isn't some mean dictator who tells us to obey without giving us any idea how. If you want to please the Lord, you absolutely can. God will help you do it.

Second, Ephesians 5:10 indicates pleasing the Lord is something we have to *learn*. Wouldn't it be nice if the moment we trusted Jesus for salvation we immediately had all the answers for life's questions? We never wanted to sin again? But if those things were true, we probably wouldn't live every day like we needed Jesus. And the truth is, *we need Jesus*.

When it comes to pleasing the Lord, Psalm 147:11 gives us a good place to start:

> *The Lord favors those who fear Him and*
> *those who wait for His loving-kindness.*

To be clear, our works do not save us. Only faith in Jesus does. But that faith is proven by whether our lives begin to change for the better. See, the more we know and love God, the more we want to obey Him. And the more we obey Him, the more we please Him.

And when we're truly pleasing God, we don't need to worry about pleasing anyone else.

¡ASPIRE TO KNOW MORE

▶ Find Hebrews 11:6. What is the first thing we need to please God?

▶ Galatians 1:10 asks a very important question that we should ask ourselves. What is it?

▶ Read Romans 8:8. Who cannot please God?

iASPIRE TO GROW IN CHRIST

*Grow in the loving-favor that Christ gives you. Learn to know
our Lord Jesus Christ better. He is the One Who saves. May He
have all the shining-greatness now and forever. Let it be so.*

2 PETER 3:18

To be a Christian is far more than simply praying the "sinner's prayer" in order to go to heaven someday. To be a Christian is to spend the rest of your life *learning Christ.*

It's easy for Christians to get distracted by what we don't know or can't understand. People love debating and arguing details of scripture that matter far less than the real goal: knowing Jesus and growing in Christlikeness.

So how do we grow in Christ? The apostle John reports that we must *abide* in Him.

"Abiding in Christ" is a biblical idea that means we remain in Jesus. We lean into Him and His wisdom. We recognize that everything in our lives comes from His hand. Abiding in Christ is believing, resting, and trusting in Jesus for everything.

Speaking of Himself, Jesus said,

> *"I am the Vine and you are the branches. Get your
> life from Me. Then I will live in you and you will give
> much fruit. You can do nothing without Me."*

JOHN 15:5

To grow in Christ is to learn the difficult but necessary task of walking by faith and not by feeling. It's trusting God and His will even when trusting doesn't seem to make sense.

Thankfully, God gives us everything we need to grow in our faith.

Growing in Christ is a wonderful process, but it takes work. Spiritual growth doesn't happen by accident. And unfortunately, there is no quick path to growth.

It's a lot like building muscle—it takes time, effort, and patience. We must make our growth a priority and not just think about it when it's convenient.

Thankfully, God gives us many ways to grow. Just like the major food groups help us grow physically, there are disciplines to help us grow spiritually. Here are some of them: reading the Bible, memorizing scripture, confessing our sin, offering thanksgiving to God, praising Him through worship, and sharing the good news of Jesus with those around us.

The more we grow in Christ, the more we begin to look like Jesus and reflect His character. The more we grow in Him, the less we look and act like unbelievers.

Growing in Christ is a process that will last your entire life. But it's absolutely worth it.

iASPIRE TO KNOW MORE

▶ Find 2 Peter 1:3. According to this verse, what does God give us for life and holy living?

▶ Looking at the list of spiritual "disciplines" above, what is one thing you can ask God to help you do more of this week?

▶ Read John 15:8. What is the ultimate goal of abiding in Christ and "bearing fruit" for Him?

¡ASPIRE TO STUDY THE BIBLE

All the Holy Writings are God-given and are made alive
by Him. Man is helped when he is taught God's Word.
It shows what is wrong. It changes the way of a man's
life. It shows him how to be right with God.

2 TIMOTHY 3:16

Your Bible is more than a rule book—it's a road map of radical transformation that changes you from the inside out. In fact, it's the most powerful book in the world.

Here's what the Bible says about itself:

God's Word is living and powerful. It is sharper than
a sword that cuts both ways. It cuts straight into where
the soul and spirit meet and it divides them. It cuts
into the joints and bones. It tells what the heart is
thinking about and what it wants to do.

HEBREWS 4:12

Have you ever heard of any other book that's *alive*? Your Bible is a living, breathing information source unlike any other. The best decision you could make is to study it carefully.

Yes, it's good to *read* the Bible. But we should all aspire to *studying* it.

Reading the Bible is simply skimming the text like you would any other printed material—a website, a magazine, a novel. Our casual reading typically moves at a good pace.

Studying the Bible, though, is reading it slowly, rereading, asking questions, and putting pieces together. When you study, you don't move on to a new verse or chapter until you truly understand what you have just read.

It doesn't matter if you're a theologian or this is the first time you've opened a Bible. God inspired His Word to be deeply meaningful for anybody who truly wants to know and obey Him.

Never look at Bible reading as simply a duty. In fact, God never commanded us to read just to check something off a list—or to be proud of finishing such a big book. No, God calls us to love His Word. He tells us that by knowing His Word, we can ultimately get to know and love *Him*:

> *I love those who love me, and those who look*
> *for me with much desire will find me.*
> PROVERBS 8:17

Not sure where to start? There are many wonderful Bible reading programs to choose from—but don't get overwhelmed by the thought of following a schedule. God doesn't command any specific plan or even to read the whole Bible in a year. Schedules can be helpful, but too many people fall behind and then stop reading entirely.

So here's the best plan: *just read and study the Bible every day*. You don't have to spend hours. Just make sure you spend some time with God's Word. If you do, you're right on time and right where you need to be for God to communicate His truth to you.

Pick up your iAspire Study Bible and just start reading. Or, if it's easier for you, press play on an audio Bible app to listen to God's Word.

Just make sure you do something.

---

iASPIRE TO KNOW MORE

▶ Find Psalm 119. Look for the many benefits that come with studying God's Word.

▶ Read Isaiah 40:8. How long does this verse say God's Word will last?

▶ One way to faithfully study God's Word is to find a time that works well in your daily schedule, then commit to spend it with your Bible. Take a few minutes to think what that time might be.

iASPIRE TO MEMORIZE SCRIPTURE

Thy word have I hid in mine heart,
that I might not sin against thee.
PSALM 119:11 KJV

When Jesus was tempted in the wilderness, what did He do?

Did He use a magic formula to fight sin?

Did He simply ignore the problem until it went away?

Did He use His best arguments and quickest comebacks to argue with the devil?

No. Jesus fought temptation *by quoting scripture*. So should we.

But how can we quote Bible verses if we don't memorize them? How can we expect God to bring verses to our mind if we haven't taken the time to put those verses in our heart?

We don't memorize scripture just because it's a spiritual discipline. We don't memorize verses just to win contests at summer camp or impress others with our Bible knowledge. The reason is far more practical: we memorize God's Word so we have the right answers at the right times.

In moments of temptation or when we're deep in conversation with someone who needs to hear the words of God, the Holy Spirit will often take verses we've hidden in our hearts and bring them to our minds clearly. Talk to someone who's been saved for many years, and most likely he or she will tell you about a time a verse "popped into my head" at the exact moment it was needed.

How does that happen? Well, the Holy Spirit brings His truth to mind. But it all begins with simple memorization.

When we "hide" God's Word in our hearts, we're preparing for future battles—battles of the mind, battles of the flesh, battles against evil in the world. The older you get, the more of these battles you'll face. It may sound dramatic referring to "future battles," but here's how God's Word describes life in this world:

> *Our fight is not with people. It is against the leaders and the powers and the spirits of darkness in this world. It is against the demon world that works in the heavens.*
>
> EPHESIANS 6:12

Also in Ephesians 6, we're instructed to put on the "armor of God." And we're to take up our sword, which is God's Word (v. 17).

God has given us a weapon to fight the battles of this life. The world is really that bad. Memorize God's Word to make it through alive!

¡ASPIRE TO KNOW MORE

▶ Find Matthew 4:1–11 for the story of Jesus' temptation in the wilderness. What can we learn from His interaction with Satan?

▶ Romans is a good book of the Bible to memorize from. Chapter 8 is filled with great verses!

▶ One way to get better at memorizing is to find a Bible memory partner. Set goals and quote verses back and forth to keep each other on track.

19

¡ASPIRE TO THINK CAREFULLY

Look through me, O God, and know my heart.
Try me and know my thoughts.
PSALM 139:23

Today, you will listen more to yourself than to any other person.

Researchers say we have between 9,000 and 60,000 thoughts each day. As many as 70 percent of those thoughts will be negative and 85 percent repetitive—meaning you had many of the same thoughts yesterday, and you'll likely have many of the very same thoughts tomorrow.

This research is really only catching up to what the Bible has already said: what you think matters. Your *thoughts* are your greatest influence.

Imagine if someone told you hundreds of times a day that you don't matter. . .that God isn't good. . .that you should only do what makes you happy. Do you think those comments would affect you over time? Of course they would! As human beings, we're wired to respond to what we hear. Your thoughts have the same incredible power to impact you, either for good or evil.

Throughout the Bible, God tells us how important our thoughts are in life. Here's an example:

Take hold of every thought and make it obey Christ.
2 CORINTHIANS 10:5

Other translations of this verse say, "Take every thought captive." These words mean we have both the responsibility and the power to control what we think. And, specifically, we should treat our thoughts like they are our prisoners. *We're* in control of our thoughts—our thoughts shouldn't control us.

The Bible tells us to guard our minds from unhelpful or unholy thoughts. And God, through the apostle Paul, gave us a helpful list through which we can filter everything we think:

> *Whatever is true, whatever is noble, whatever*
> *is right, whatever is pure, whatever is lovely,*
> *whatever is admirable—if anything is excellent*
> *or praiseworthy—think about such things.*
>
> PHILIPPIANS 4:8 NIV

Perhaps the reason God tells us to control our thinking is because our thoughts shape us. *We become what we think.*

A popular quotation captures this idea well. "Watch your thoughts, they become your words; watch your words, they become your actions; watch your actions, they become your habits; watch your habits, they become your character; watch your character, it becomes your destiny."

If you want to make good choices with your life, start by making good choices with your thoughts. Aspire to think carefully.

¡ASPIRE TO KNOW MORE

▶ Pay close attention to your thoughts today. How often do you think about negative or unhelpful things? Each time you catch yourself thinking this way, stop and ask God to help you. He will.

▶ Find Romans 12:2. According to this verse, when God changes your life, what does He change first?

▶ Read Proverbs 23:7 in the New Life or King James Versions of the Bible. What do your thoughts affect?

¡ASPIRE TO MAKE GOOD CHOICES

Do not act like the sinful people of the world. Let God change your life. First of all, let Him give you a new mind. Then you will know what God wants you to do. And the things you do will be good and pleasing and perfect.

ROMANS 12:2

We can sometimes be tempted to think our choices aren't a big deal. Maybe we think our daily decisions only affect us.

▶ Is it really a problem to cheat on a quiz?
▶ Does anyone get hurt if I tell a little lie to stay out of trouble?
▶ Who would even know or care if I steal something small?

But every decision has consequences.

A *consequence* is something that results from a choice we make. Consequences themselves aren't negative or positive—they're simply the aftereffect of our decisions.

The Old Testament story of Joseph clearly shows that even our small choices can have big consequences and that our choices always affect other people.

Consider the various decisions throughout the story: Joseph wears the special coat his doting father gives him, even though it upsets his older brothers; Joseph is sold as a slave into Egypt but serves his owner, Potiphar, in a way that glorifies God; Joseph resists the sexual temptation of Potiphar's wife, though that gets him thrown into prison; while incarcerated, Joseph is faithful to God and helpful to others, which ultimately propels him into leadership over all Egypt.

Every one of Joseph's choices impacted his life. And his choices ultimately led the entire clan of Israel to move to Egypt, where they would stay for 430 years. That fulfilled a promise God made to Abraham in Genesis 15.

There is no such thing as a choice without consequences. Those consequences can be good or bad, depending on the choices you make. You have the freedom to make poor choices—*but you don't have power over their consequences.*

When he was a teenager, Joseph probably gave little thought to the way his choices would affect others. He may have assumed—as we sometimes do—that they only affected him.

By Genesis 50 though, Joseph was a grown man who seemed to understand the importance of choices. When he got an opportunity to confront his brothers—who had hated him and sold him into slavery—he chose kindness over revenge. Though Joseph could have had the men killed, he didn't even yell at them. Instead, he said,

> *"You planned to do a bad thing to me. But God planned it for good, to make it happen that many people should be kept alive, as they are today."*
> GENESIS 50:20

Better choices lead to better consequences. And when we aspire to please the Lord with our choices, He will work out even the *bad* choices of other people for our good (Romans 8:28).

¡ASPIRE TO KNOW MORE

▶ Look up Genesis 37, where Joseph is seventeen years old. Read this chapter and underline all the choices he made. Keep in mind, these choices would affect the rest of his life.

▶ Today you will be faced with choices. Pray and ask God to help you choose correctly.

iASPIRE TO LOVE WHAT IS PURE

Do not be guilty of telling bad stories and of foolish talk.
These things are not for you to do. Instead, you are to
give thanks for what God has done for you.

EPHESIANS 5:4

God wants more than just your good behavior—He wants your heart.

As we read the Bible, we learn that God isn't concerned with our outward appearance. That is, He doesn't just want us to "clean up our act." He wants us to have a clean heart.

Not doing bad things isn't enough—God wants us to *desire good things*.

Having good desires is infinitely harder than doing good things. Why? Because we can "go through the motions" of good behavior while secretly enjoying sinful things.

In Matthew 23, Jesus talks to a group of proud religious leaders known as scribes and Pharisees. These men were enemies to the true Gospel of Jesus, and He knew it. The scribes and Pharisees were known for looking good on the outside while being evil inside. They loved to look pure without loving what was pure.

To prove He knew their hearts, Jesus started giving them illustrations like this: imagine going to somebody's house for supper and being served the most delicious-looking food on a disgusting, dirty plate. Or imagine you reach for your drink—in a clean, shiny silver goblet—only to find the most rancid milk inside. Would you want to eat or drink those things? Of course not!

Jesus is frustrated by people who look good on the outside but are filthy inside. Here's what He said to the Pharisees:

> *"It is bad for you, teachers of the Law and proud*
> *religious law-keepers, you who pretend to be someone*

you are not! You clean the outside of the cup and plate,
but leave the inside full of strong bad desires and are not
able to keep from doing sinful things. You blind proud
religious law-keepers! Clean the inside of the cup
and plate, then the outside will be clean also."

MATTHEW 23:25–26

Loving what is pure requires much more than wearing the right clothes, listening to the right music, and knowing the right answers in Sunday school. Loving what is pure requires much more than simply being known as "a good kid." Loving what is pure means we genuinely love what God loves—and hate what He hates.

Colossians 3:5 tells us to "destroy the desires to sin that are in you." This is a lifelong process that requires our full attention.

Don't be like the Pharisees, who looked like silver goblets but were full of spoiled milk.

¡ASPIRE TO KNOW MORE

▶ Find Matthew 23:13–33. Read more of the conversation Jesus had with the Pharisees and scribes.

▶ Why do you think Jesus had less patience for the scribes and Pharisees than He did for other sinners He came across? (Hint: read Matthew 23:13.)

iASPIRE TO USE MY TIME WISELY

Make the best use of your time.
These are sinful days.
EPHESIANS 5:16

The world is full of distractions. For every task you should complete today, you have a dozen options that probably sound like more fun.

Maybe you enjoy playing video games or listening to music. Maybe you like texting your friends or surfing the Internet. God has kindly given us many things to enjoy in this life—but He always wants us to make wise choices.

One way we grow spiritually is by learning to use our time wisely. Just like money, we have a limited amount of time to spend. What we do with it matters.

What if we learned to spend our time more carefully by categorizing every potential choice as *good*, *better*, or *best*?

Good choices might include playing games or going shopping.

Better choices might include spending time with friends or reading good books.

Best choices might include serving others or studying the Bible.

Only God can help us know what choices fit in each category. We should ask for wisdom, praying the words of Psalm 90:12:

Teach us to understand how many days we have.
Then we will have a heart of wisdom to give You.

Growing in wisdom includes learning to say *no* to good things so we'll have time to say *yes* to the best things. For example, reading your Bible, attending church, sharing the Gospel, and serving your family are nonnegotiables in the Christian life. (A "nonnegotiable" is something that isn't open for debate.)

When God's Word specifically tells us to do something, the decision to obey is the best choice we can make. Everything else needs to fit into the Bible's framework.

Are sports bad? No. . .but they shouldn't be a reason we regularly skip going to church.

Are movies bad? No. . .but they shouldn't keep us from prayer.

Are friends bad? No. . .but they shouldn't interfere with our other duties to God.

So how do we learn to use time wisely?

To aspire to use our time wisely, we must understand that life is short and eternity is forever. We'll never regret spending our time doing things that count for eternity, even if we have to give up some fun choices in the meantime.

No matter what, the best use of our time is to love and serve the Lord.

¡ASPIRE TO KNOW MORE

▶ Find 2 Corinthians 4:18. According to this verse, what are the things that last forever?

▶ Read Proverbs 6:6–8. What does God say we should look at when we're tempted to be lazy? What are we supposed to learn from her?

▶ What is an example of a *good, better,* and *best* decision in your life?

iASPIRE TO ASK FOR HELP

If you do not have wisdom, ask God for it.
He is always ready to give it to you and
will never say you are wrong for asking.

JAMES 1:5

Sometimes the bravest, wisest thing you can do is ask for help.

If you have a need or you're struggling under the weight of a specific fear, temptation, or sin, asking for help is always the right decision.

Sometimes we're scared to ask for help because we don't want people to see our weakness. We want people to believe we're stronger than we really are. Sometimes we forget that *every* human being has struggles and temptations just like we do. But struggling silently is one of the worst things we can do.

Satan wants us to keep our struggles a secret—because when we do, those struggles control us. They affect the way we think, the way we speak, and the way we act. Often, these struggles even control whether we pray and worship God the way we should. They're like heavy chains around our ankles, keeping us from running our race to the glory of God.

That is not God's desire for you.

So He has put people in your life to help you when you need it. Even better, God Himself wants to help when you're struggling.

In the Old Testament, the name *Elohim* is used over two thousand times. It's a Hebrew name for God that means "strength." *Our God is mighty in strength.* He is more than able to help with your deepest needs, whatever they are.

Start with God, every time, in prayer. Then go to the people He has put in your life, and draw from their strength.

If you have parents, grandparents, or great-grandparents who love

God, go to them. Tell them what you're facing (and feeling) in your life. Ask for their help. Then take time to listen to what they say. Your older family members have already lived more life (and made more instructive mistakes) than you have. And while they may not understand everything about being a teenager today, they probably get way more than you think. And they'll probably be happy to share some lessons they learned at your age.

When you need help, the worst thing you can do is hide that fact from the people who love you or from God. He already knows!

George Müller, a man who cared for more than ten thousand orphans in the 1800s, said, "Be assured, if you walk with [God] and look to Him, and expect help from Him, He will never fail you."

¡ASPIRE TO KNOW MORE

▶ Find 1 Peter 5:7. Why does God invite us to give our worries to Him?

▶ Do you need to ask for help with some struggle in your life? Take the first step and pray for wisdom. And ask God to show you someone to talk to.

24

¡ASPIRE TO DEAL WITH DOUBT

You must have faith as you ask Him. You must not doubt. Anyone who doubts is like a wave which is pushed around by the sea.

JAMES 1:6

What if everything Jesus said really is true?

Nicodemus was a successful, intelligent man. A member of the Jewish ruling council, he personally watched Jesus and listened to what He said. And like many people of his day, Nicodemus had doubts. He knew what the religious leaders said about Jesus—the fact that they were calling Him a liar and a lunatic. He knew that people even wanted Jesus dead. And yet, Nicodemus couldn't stop thinking about this man who was changing lives.

So, under cover of darkness, Nicodemus did the wisest thing possible: he took his doubts and questions directly to Jesus.

In the night hours, the two men talked. And when Nicodemus asked questions, Jesus responded with kindness and compassion. In fact, the most famous Bible verse of all—John 3:16—is something Jesus spoke to this man:

> *"For God so loved the world that He gave His only Son. Whoever puts his trust in God's Son will not be lost but will have life that lasts forever."*

Jesus didn't badger or belittle Nicodemus. But the Lord clearly and unapologetically gave him the only truth that was sufficient to deal with his greatest doubts.

Jesus shared the Gospel.

Doubts aren't really our problem. Doubts actually reflect our heart's desire to know the truth.

Most of us don't lie awake at night wondering if Santa Claus or the Easter Bunny are actually real. Do we even really care? But Jesus. . .that's a whole different story. We know in our hearts that He is real, and His claims on our life are valid. In fact, we were *created* to know this truth.

It's what we do with our doubts that makes a difference.

Doing nothing or going to the wrong place for answers can be devastating to life and eternity. If Nicodemus had taken his doubts to the other religious leaders—those men who hated Jesus and wanted to kill Him—he would have received the wrong answers. But Nicodemus did what we should do with our doubts: he took them to Jesus Himself.

When you have doubts about God or His Word (and we all do at some time or another), the wisest thing you can do is take them to God in prayer. After that, find someone you trust who clearly and consistently walks with God. Maybe that's a pastor, a teacher, a parent, or a friend. Ask for one-on-one time, and carefully share what you're thinking. Listen carefully to their response, and compare everything you hear to God's Word. He will help you through your doubts in His own way and time.

Don't stop believing.

¡ASPIRE TO KNOW MORE

▶ Find John 3:15. What did Jesus tell Nicodemus will happen to those who trust in Him?

▶ Read John 19:38–40. What did Nicodemus do after Jesus died on the cross?

25

¡ASPIRE TO PRAY OFTEN

Do not worry. Learn to pray about everything.
Give thanks to God as you ask Him for what you need.
PHILIPPIANS 4:6

You have no greater privilege than to talk to God. In fact, if the president of the United States wanted to call and talk to you on the phone today, it would still be a greater privilege to talk to God. He owns the universe!

If you are a child of God, you have a gracious, loving, heavenly Father who invites you to bring everything to Him in prayer. Stop and think about that. Isn't it amazing?

When we truly understand what prayer is—a direct line of communication with our Creator—we begin to see prayer for the enormous gift that it is. God doesn't owe us the privilege of prayer, but He gives it to us freely.

Are you nervous about a test at school? Talk to God.

Do you feel lonely or misunderstood? Talk to God.

Are you curious or scared about your future? Talk to God.

He knows everything, and He invites you to share your heart with Him.

In the Old Testament, the Lord came to Jeremiah and said,

> *"Call to Me, and I will answer you. And I will show you great*
> *and wonderful things which you do not know."*
> JEREMIAH 33:3

And God invites you to do the same.

If we're honest with ourselves, we might have to admit that the greatest obstacle to answered prayer is actually *unoffered* prayer. We may say our prayers aren't being answered, but if we take a good look at our prayer life, we might find that we aren't actually praying that often. Prayer—though it is a gift—is still a discipline that takes effort and honesty on our part. The hardest part of praying is simply getting started.

God invites us to come often and to come boldly. But keep this in mind: the main reason we pray isn't so that we get things—even good things—from God. We pray to put ourselves in our rightful place and to acknowledge God in *His*. He is in charge of everything, and our job is to submit to His will.

The God of the Bible isn't distant. He isn't too big or too busy to care about the details of your life. He's close and personal. He loves you and wants you to talk to Him.

So if you're ever at a loss for words when life is hard, you can borrow the words spoken of the prophet Jeremiah: "O Lord God! See, You have made the heavens and the earth by Your great power and by Your long arm! Nothing is too hard for You!" (Jeremiah 32:17).

¡ASPIRE TO KNOW MORE

▶ What do you need to talk to God about? Stop and pray right now.

▶ Find Psalm 145:18. Where is God when you pray to Him?

▶ Read 1 Thessalonians 5:17. How often are we supposed to pray?

26

¡ASPIRE TO HATE SIN

Be sure your love is true love. Hate what is sinful.
Hold on to whatever is good.

ROMANS 12:9

Every sinful choice begins with believing a lie. And here is that lie: *you need something else in order to be happy.*

And, to be honest, our sinful choices often feel good, at least for a fleeting moment. But sin blinds us to the promises of God—including the fact that He has already given us *everything* we need—and sin always ends up robbing us blind.

So what exactly is sin? Any thought, feeling, or action that doesn't please God.

Sin will steal your joy, your peace, and your contentment. Sin will stand between you and your God. Sin will stunt your spiritual growth and ruin your relationships. And if it isn't handled correctly, sin will destroy you.

Sin always comes with a price, and the price is always more than you want to pay:

But each person is tempted when they are dragged
away by their own evil desire and enticed. Then,
after desire has conceived, it gives birth to sin; and sin,
when it is full-grown, gives birth to death.

JAMES 1:14–15 NIV

The very first sin occurred when Eve ate the fruit that God commanded her not to eat. She fell into the trap that we all do: every sin represents the human belief that *we know better than God does.*

In the Garden of Eden, the serpent said to Eve, "You will not surely die"—even though God had clearly said the opposite. But Eve was eager to believe that the serpent (and she) knew better than God.

When we sin, we do the same thing. Every sin—at its core—is wrong thinking about God. The problem is that we *don't* know better than God knows. Eventually, we recognize that fact. But it's up to us whether we acknowledge that truth in faith before we sin or with consequences afterward.

Here's the good news: *you always have a choice.* You don't need to sin! God has given you His Word and His Holy Spirit to help you fight every temptation to sin. You have all you need. Pray. Quote scripture. Ask your parents or mentors for support. God will always help you.

No matter how attractive sinful choices look, we must always think of our sin in terms of what it cost Jesus. We can't say that we love Him if we also love the sin that put Him on the cross.

A seventeenth-century pastor, Thomas Watson, said, "Christ is never loved until sin is loathed." But don't trust your own heart with regard to sin. Our flesh is not our friend, and to truly fight sin, we must consistently remain suspicious of our own motives. Step one: stop believing you're strong enough to handle temptation on your own.

Today and every day, we must aspire to hate sin. Ask God to give you more love for Him than for anything this world offers.

¡ASPIRE TO KNOW MORE

▶ What is the simple definition of sin found in 1 John 5:17?

▶ The unfortunate reality is that we *will* sin because we are all sinners. But is it possible for a true believer to consistently sin without feeling bad about it? Read 1 John 3:9.

▶ Next time you are tempted to think, say, or do something sinful, interrupt yourself with these words: "I have a choice." Then pray and ask God to help you choose correctly.

iASPIRE TO RECOGNIZE PRIDE

When pride comes, then comes shame,
but wisdom is with those who have no pride.
PROVERBS 11:2

Pride is at the root of every sin and evil in the world.

Pride is a form of self-worship that starts in the heart. It is the reason we enjoy finding faults in other people. It's the reason we're unthoughtful or dishonest. It's the reason we're defensive or fake. When pride rears its ugly head, we make ourselves the god of our own universe, and suddenly *our* opinions, *our* desires, and *our* plans matter more than anyone else's.

Pride is the reason Adam and Eve sinned in the Garden of Eden. It's the reason Cain killed his brother, Abel. It's the reason Jonah ran from Nineveh. It's the reason the Romans crucified Jesus.

And it's the reason behind every sin we commit today.

Pride isn't God's desire, which is why the single greatest superpower in the Christian life is humility. Humility is the opposite of pride. It's what we need in order to come to Christ for salvation. It's also what we need so God can change us to be more like His Son.

Humility recognizes God in His rightful place and keeps us in ours.

But humility is one of the most *unnatural* things in the world. Our culture tells us to be loud and proud about who we are and what we want. Our own proud hearts naturally crave the applause of men far more than approval of God.

But what does the Bible say?

Nothing should be done because of pride
or thinking about yourself. Think of other
people as more important than yourself.
PHILIPPIANS 2:3

What happens when we think of others as more important than ourselves? We love them, serve them, show grace to them, and bear patiently with them. We share the truth of the Gospel with them because we want them to know that Jesus loves them too. We don't easily get our feelings hurt. We don't need popularity or praise. We don't live for the approval of anybody but God. In other words, killing pride and choosing humility is *freedom*!

Humility causes us to love *other people* as much as pride causes us to love *ourselves*. Now, in case you think humility sounds too harsh or drab, know that there is a reward for lowering ourselves in our own estimation: God "gives His loving-favor to those who do not try to honor themselves" (1 Peter 5:5).

¡ASPIRE TO KNOW MORE

▶ Jeremiah 9:23–24 says there is only one thing we have the right to be proud of. What is it?

▶ One easy way to fight pride is to pray. Prayer is the way we recognize God as Lord and lean on Him instead of ourselves. Have you prayed today? If you want God's help identifying and removing pride from your heart, pray the words of Psalm 139:23–24 to God.

28

¡ASPIRE TO FIGHT SELFISHNESS

*Nothing should be done because of pride or
thinking about yourself. Think of other people
as more important than yourself.*
<small>PHILIPPIANS 2:3</small>

What have you done today to help somebody else?

Maybe you don't have a car you can use to take an elderly neighbor to the doctor. Maybe you don't have a lot of money to give to the needy. Maybe you just don't think you have the right personality to step up and help. But the truth is, God has specifically equipped you with certain abilities and talents to love and serve others.

When we're consumed with ourselves—what *we* feel, what *we're* experiencing, what *we* want—we're being selfish. And when we're selfish, we're not able to think of others or serve them as God intends. Selfishness contaminates our motives and cripples our character.

In fact, when we're being selfish, we look the least like Jesus:

*Do not always be thinking about your own plans only.
Be happy to know what other people are doing. Think as
Christ Jesus thought. Jesus has always been as God is.
But He did not hold to His rights as God. He put aside
everything that belonged to Him and made Himself the same
as a servant who is owned by someone. He became human
by being born as a man. After He became a man, He gave up
His important place and obeyed by dying on a cross.*
<small>PHILIPPIANS 2:4-8</small>

If Jesus—who had every right to think of Himself—chose instead to think of others, shouldn't we do the same? Thankfully, there are many ways you can love and serve other people today:

- ▶ Look for someone at school, church, or work who is being ignored, and talk to that person instead of your closer friends.
- ▶ Ask someone how he or she is doing and then truly listen to the answer.
- ▶ Write a note or send a text to someone who needs encouragement.
- ▶ Find ways to be helpful at home. Can you offer to set the table or help with laundry?
- ▶ Next time you hear about an event at school or church, ask the person in charge if there is anything you can do to help.

But remember: don't do any of these things hoping to be praised or thanked. Serve to be like Jesus. God will help you. Ask Him for courage and strength to do a good job, because He is happy to answer prayers like that. "If a man helps others, let him do it with the strength God gives. So in all things God may be honored through Jesus Christ" (1 Peter 4:11).

Fighting selfishness is a lifelong job, but it's a job worth doing for the glory of God.

¡ASPIRE TO KNOW MORE

- ▶ Find Romans 12:15. This is a short verse, but it's a powerful description of what it looks like to live unselfishly.

- ▶ Think of something you're good at doing. How can you use a strength or talent God has given you to help another person this week?

29

¡ASPIRE TO DENY MYSELF

*Jesus said to His followers, "If anyone wants to
be My follower, he must forget about himself.
He must take up his cross and follow Me."*
MATTHEW 16:24

Deny yourself.

This is an instruction you won't find anywhere in the world except your Bible. In fact, the world will tell you just the opposite. Culture says to make yourself number one. It'll encourage you to follow your heart, do whatever makes you happy, and always remember that *you are enough*.

But as a follower of Christ, you know better. You know, for example, that *God* is number one, that your heart is *deceptive*, and that *Jesus* is enough.

And Jesus' way is always better.

Based on what we read in scripture, we have a duty and a privilege to deny ourselves and follow Christ. But what does denying ourselves look like?

▶ It looks like treasuring God's opinion more than we value the opinion of people.
▶ It looks like desiring to make God famous instead of making ourselves famous.
▶ It looks like choosing God and His Will over our own comfort.

In multiple places throughout your Bible, Jesus is recorded as saying words like these:

*"If anyone wants to follow Me, he must give
up himself and his own desires. He must take
up his cross every day and follow Me."*
LUKE 9:23

When Jesus commands that you deny yourself and follow Him, He isn't just trying to take away all your fun. He isn't a mean guy who wants to see you sad or bored. Jesus is actually inviting you to live a life of greater joy and satisfaction *in Him*.

Jesus knows that things like money, friends, movies, music, sex, and alcohol can only make you happy for a short time. But a relationship with Him—creating a mind-set of surrender and service in this life—can bring unlimited joy for eternity. It's actually a gracious command from God to leave all of earth's pleasures behind to chase after His Son!

Here's a remarkable promise you can hang onto: Jesus is worth anything and everything you set aside in order to follow Him. So, for example, if God calls you into full-time ministry instead of a high-paying career—and you obey that calling—Jesus will be worth every penny you don't make, every achievement you don't earn, and every promotion you don't receive.

If you choose Jesus over attending parties that don't glorify God, over dating people who aren't followers of Christ, and over making decisions with your future based entirely on human success, Jesus will be worth every moment of discomfort you have in accepting your reality.

Why? Because He will be with you—and for the person who truly learns to love Jesus more than anything or anyone in this life, *that is enough*.

Jesus is always enough.

¡ASPIRE TO KNOW MORE

▶ Find John 12:24-26. What is the example Jesus gives in these verses of something that dies in order to become something even better?

▶ In John 10:10, Jesus shares His true motive coming to earth. What is it?

30

¡ASPIRE TO RESIST TEMPTATION

*You have never been tempted to sin in any different way than
other people. God is faithful. He will not allow you to be
tempted more than you can take. But when you are tempted,
He will make a way for you to keep from falling into sin.*

1 CORINTHIANS 10:13

Much of our temptation in life can be traced to desires that are good. For example, if you're tempted to cheat on a test at school, the ultimate desire may be to earn a good grade or to please your teacher or to avoid trouble at home. Those desires, of themselves, are not wrong.

Desires become sinful when we want to achieve them by following our own plan instead of doing things God's way. So the best way to fight temptation isn't to stop wanting things—it's to love God and His Word even more than you want to follow your own path.

When Jesus was thirty years old—right after He was baptized and publicly identified as the Son of God—He was led by the Holy Spirit into the desert. For forty days He had nothing to eat. As you can imagine, Jesus was hungry and uncomfortable—and Satan chose this as the time to tempt Him. In fact, the Bible tells us that Satan tempted Jesus *throughout* the forty days of solitude and fasting. The devil was committed to making Jesus sin and canceling His plan to die for the sins of the world.

Matthew 4 records three ways Satan tempted Jesus:

▶ *"If You are the Son of God, tell these stones to be made into bread"* (v. 3).
▶ *"If You are the Son of God, throw Yourself down [from the temple roof]"* (v. 6).
▶ *"I will give You all these nations if You will get down at my feet and worship me"* (v. 9).

In all three of these temptations, Satan used the word *if*. He does the same when he tempts *you* to sin. He encourages you to question what you already know to be true about God. If Satan can get you to question God and His Word, you can commit *any* sin. And that's right where Satan wants you to be.

The good news is that you don't need to fight temptation in your own strength. God is committed to helping you make right choices.

Just like Jesus did in the wilderness, you can fight every sinful temptation that comes your way. How? In each of His own temptations, Jesus responded by quoting scripture—and you can do the same.

Today and every day, God has promised to provide you with a holy alternative to every sinful choice you may be tempted to make. Why not take Him up on His offer?

¡ASPIRE TO KNOW MORE

▶ Find Matthew 4:1-11 to read the full story of Jesus being tempted.

▶ Find Genesis 3:1-6 to read the story of the first temptation in human history.

▶ How are these two stories about temptation different?

31

¡ASPIRE TO ADMIT WHEN I'M WRONG

If we tell Him our sins, He is faithful and we can depend on Him to
forgive us of our sins. He will make our lives clean from all sin.

1 JOHN 1:9

Everybody messes up.

Any human being who is not Jesus has made mistakes. We're not sinners because we sin; we sin because we're sinners. That may not seem like a big difference, but it is. We sin because it's in our DNA. By the time you learned what sin was, you had already sinned more times than you could count!

So. . .since we know we're sinners who sin, we should be quick to admit when we're wrong. And we should be ready to make things right.

The word for that is *repentance*. It includes telling someone you were wrong, asking for that person's forgiveness, and then making a change in your behavior.

The Bible says a lot about repentance, specifically that it's a wise thing to do:

> *It will not go well for the man who hides his sins, but he who*
> *tells his sins and turns from them will be given loving-pity.*
> PROVERBS 28:13

Even though we know it's the right thing to do, admitting we're wrong is often one of the hardest things to do. But it's also one of the best things we can do, because what God desires most from us is that we are humble and obedient to Him.

If you notice that you're making a lot of wrong choices that require you to ask forgiveness, stop and evaluate your walk with God. Sin is a good indicator of what we need to better understand about God. For example, if you're regularly unkind to people, that shows you don't yet understand how kind God has been to you. If you're failing to trust God the way you should, you don't yet understand how trustworthy He is.

Our sinful choices reveal what we truly believe.

So what is the right way to admit we're wrong?

Confessing sin means that we acknowledge the poor choice we've made without trying to minimize, rationalize, or excuse it. This can be difficult to do. Sometimes other people had something to do with our wrong choice. Maybe another person came up with the bad idea or encouraged us to do the wrong thing. But admitting we're wrong means taking responsibility for our participation.

You don't have to prepare a big speech or write a long letter. You don't have to be dramatic or emotional. You simply have to say you're sorry *and mean it*. It can be hard in the moment, but admitting when we're wrong is always the right decision.

¡ASPIRE TO KNOW MORE

▶ Find 1 John 1:8. What does the Bible say about someone who says he doesn't sin?

▶ Read Psalm 86:5. According to this verse, God is ready to forgive and is rich in loving-kindness to whom?

32

¡ASPIRE TO ASK FOR FORGIVENESS

The gifts on an altar that God wants are a broken spirit. O God,
You will not hate a broken heart and a heart with no pride.

PSALM 51:17

It takes courage to ask forgiveness when you're wrong.

Without a doubt, *all* of us make wrong choices. We're *all* sinful human beings. But not *all* of us know how to make things right.

Repentance can be the difference between life and death, between a future and no future.

Consider the life of David from the Old Testament. He did big things for God. He killed Goliath. He was king of Israel for forty years. He wrote many of the psalms. But David also made some terrible decisions. He stole a man's wife and took the man's life—two of the worst choices he could possibly have made!

So why on earth is David called "a man after [God's] own heart"? (See 1 Samuel 13:14 NIV and Acts 13:22 NIV.) The answer: he repented and asked for forgiveness.

Repentance is confessing our sin to the person we've sinned against not so we can avoid consequences, but so we can repair what has been broken.

True repentance can change your life because it glorifies God.

David understood something about his sin that we also need to understand: *every sin is ultimately a sin against God.*

In fact, even though David hurt many people with his decisions, he still prayed,

I have sinned against You, and You only [God].
I have done what is sinful in Your eyes.

PSALM 51:4

When we've done something wrong, it may not feel like we've sinned against God. We had a run-in with a friend or a family member, or maybe someone sinned against us first. We probably never gave God a thought while we were committing the sin, so how could it be a sin against *Him*?

No matter who is involved, every sin we commit is ultimately an act of disobedience against God. Since He has told us in His Word what we're supposed to do, every violation is a sin against Him.

For example, the Bible tells us not to lie. So when we lie to a brother or sister, we're ultimately sinning against God, who told us in His Word *not* to lie.

When we confess our sin, the first person to ask forgiveness from is God. The wonderful, gracious result of confessing to Him first is that He will forgive us and then give us courage to make things right with the other people we've wronged.

Every sin is inexcusable. But by God's grace, every sin you confess is forgivable.

¡ASPIRE TO KNOW MORE

▶ Read 2 Samuel 12:13. When David realized what he had done and how he had sinned, what were the first words out of his mouth? What was the prophet Nathan's response?

▶ Is there anyone in your life from whom you need to seek forgiveness? Pray and ask God to give you courage to talk to that person today.

33

¡ASPIRE TO BE ACCOUNTABLE

Help each other in troubles and problems.
This is the kind of law Christ asks us to obey.
GALATIANS 6:2

Each one of us struggles with stubborn, sinful habits. Unfortunately, that's one of the side effects of being a sinner in a fallen world. As the apostle Paul wrote,

For all men have sinned and have
missed the shining-greatness of God.
ROMANS 3:23

Sometimes we have certain sins that just hang us up. No matter how badly we want to stop doing them or how often we ask God to forgive us, we continue to fail. It can be frustrating and defeating.

Many people call these particular sins "besetting sins," from the old King James translation of Hebrews 12:1: "the sin which doth so easily beset us." This just indicates those sins we're more likely to struggle with personally because of our circumstances or emotional makeup.

For example, some people have sinful habits of losing their temper or telling lies. Others might be lazy or look at things online that don't bring any glory to God. Whatever sin we regularly commit can be a besetting sin.

God has graciously given us a solution to our sin problem in the form of friends, parents, teachers, or mentors. If you have people in your life who love both God and you, you've been given a great gift. One of God's good plans for your life is *accountability*.

Accountability involves finding a person or two—of the same sex if at all possible—with whom you can talk openly and honestly about your walk with God. It can be as simple as checking in with each other once or twice a week to ask how the Christian life is going. You can ask each other whether you're reading your Bible and praying like you should. You can read a book (like this one!) together, and share other things God is teaching you.

Accountability can also be a promise that, when you're tempted to commit your besetting sin, you will reach out and ask for help and prayer.

This idea is much more than just confession and rebuke. Accountability is meant to encourage people, to build them up in the faith. When it's done right, accountability is life-giving and life-changing.

Imagine being ready to commit a besetting sin only to have your accountability partner pull you from the clutches of that bad decision. Suddenly, you've been encouraged to point your gaze to God. Could anything be better?

It's far worse—and much harder over time—to struggle silently with sin. Very often, the secret to success in the Christian life is accountability.

¡ASPIRE TO KNOW MORE

▶ Who in your life might make a good accountability partner? Reach out to see if he or she would be willing. If not, don't be discouraged! Keep searching until you find the right person.

▶ Find Proverbs 25:12. According to this verse, what is a wise listener like?

iASPIRE TO TRY AGAIN

*And let us not be weary in well doing: for in
due season we shall reap, if we faint not.*
GALATIANS 6:9 KJV

Ever have a bad day and wish you could have a fresh start? If so, you aren't alone.

Living the Christian life as God intended isn't easy. Nor did He promise it would be. In fact, Jesus said just the opposite:

*"If anyone wants to follow Me, he must give
up himself and his own desires. He must take
up his cross everyday and follow Me."*
LUKE 9:23

Take up a cross? That doesn't sound like fun. But fun isn't our goal. Remember, we don't follow Christ because of what we'll get out of it; we follow Christ because of what He's done for us.

The Christian life is filled with challenges and obstacles, and one of the things we must learn to do with God's grace is *fail well*. This means, when we sin, we need to handle it correctly and keep going. The worst kind of failure is quitting.

If you find yourself constantly wrestling with your flesh over what you should and shouldn't do, be encouraged. You're a lot like the apostle Paul.

The great missionary and most prolific writer in the New Testament once said this:

*I want to do what is good, but I don't. I don't want
to do what is wrong, but I do it anyway.*
ROMANS 7:19 NLT

Understand what Paul's saying? We've all been there.

But here is very good news: Jesus understands what you're facing and feeling.

He came to earth to die for our sins, and in doing so, He learned firsthand what it's like to be human. One of the kindest insights we're given in the Bible is that Jesus "understands how weak we are. Christ was tempted in every way we are tempted, but He did not sin" (Hebrews 4:15).

In other words, even though Jesus Himself never sinned, He completely understands every temptation and weakness you have. Isn't that wonderful? You get to pray to a God who understands!

So if you're having a bad day, a bad week, or a bad year and you want a new beginning, the time for that is *now*. The Bible says that every morning is a chance to start fresh: "It is because of the Lord's loving-kindness that we are not destroyed for His loving-pity never ends. It is new every morning. He is so very faithful" (Lamentations 3:22–23).

So try again.

Trust God more. Love God more. Obey God more.

And when you make a mistake, don't give up. *Try again.*

And when you know you've failed, confess it, and *try again.*

God is so very faithful.

---

iASPIRE TO KNOW MORE

▶ Find Deuteronomy 32:4. Perfection exists in only one person. Who is it?

▶ Read 2 Peter 3:9. If you are a child of God, what is His attitude toward you when you sin or make mistakes?

▶ Look up Ephesians 4:30. When Christians sin, how does God feel?

35

¡ASPIRE TO LOVE MY NEIGHBOR

You obey the whole Law when you do this one thing,
"Love your neighbor as you love yourself."
GALATIANS 5:14

One of the ways we honor God is by loving the people He created.

- ▶ Even the person who's hard to get along with.
- ▶ Even the person who's hard to understand.
- ▶ Even the person who doesn't seem to like you.

In fact, loving people isn't optional—it's required. Jesus said it's the second greatest command after this one: "You must love the Lord your God with all your heart and with all your soul and with all your mind and with all your strength" (Mark 12:30).

God could have said *anything* was the second greatest command. He could have said the second greatest command was giving our money to the church, or taking the Gospel to other countries, or controlling our temper. But the command He chose to be number two on the list was *love your neighbor.*

Love is more than just a rule to follow—it's the way we're identified as Christ-followers. It isn't normal to love everyone, so that sets us apart as belonging to God.

Dear friends, let us love each other, because love
comes from God. Those who love are God's children
and they know God. Those who do not love do
not know God because God is love.

1 JOHN 4:7–8

Have you noticed that we live in an age of outrage? People literally flip out over anything. According to statistics, more than twelve hundred car accidents end in serious injury or death every year as a direct result of road rage.

So in an era when people aren't typically kind to each other, we as Christians have an amazing opportunity to let the love of Jesus shine through us. We look the most like Christ when we love people, including and maybe even especially *when they don't deserve it.*

So how is it possible to love people who haven't earned it? Does God really expect us to love people who have been unloving toward us? The answer is found in 1 John 4:9–11: "God has shown His love to us by sending His only Son into the world. God did this so we might have life through Christ. This is love! It is not that we loved God but that He loved us. For God sent His Son to pay for our sins with His own blood. Dear friends, if God loved us that much, then we should love each other."

When we truly begin to understand how much God loves us (and how unworthy we are of His love), we'll naturally want to love other people better.

¡ASPIRE TO KNOW MORE

▶ Who do you need to love better? Ask God to show you how to be loving toward that person this week. Then do something about it.

▶ Find 1 John 4:19. What is the simple reason we should love other people?

▶ What does the next verse, 1 John 4:20, say about someone who claims to love God while hating other people?

iASPIRE TO SERVE OTHERS

Remember to do good and help each other.
Gifts like this please God.
HEBREWS 13:16

Jesus is the ultimate example of humility.

Nobody who has ever walked on this earth was more important than the Son of God. Yet nobody who has ever walked on this earth has done a better job of serving people than Jesus did.

So what exactly did Jesus do?

He put aside everything that belonged to Him and made Him-
self the same as a servant who is owned by someone.

PHILIPPIANS 2:7

Whether He was with the woman at the well (who was making bad decisions with her life) or the arrogant Jewish religious leaders (who thought they knew more than God), Jesus willingly and compassionately served everyone around him. He literally put the needs of all He met ahead of His own, even to the point of dying on the cross so we can be reconciled to God.

By His own life, Jesus proved that serving others doesn't mean you don't matter. It means you understand *who* and *what* matters most.

He also demonstrated with His life that love isn't just something we say, it's something we *do*. As children of God, we should demonstrate our love for Him every day through acts of service for others.

God hasn't called any of us to die for the sins of the world. But He does expect us to view others as more important than ourselves and to serve those around us.

Whenever you have the ability to help someone in need—whether by feeding the hungry, defending the mistreated, listening to the lonely, or helping the hurt—you should always do for that person what Jesus would do. By making the types of choices Jesus would, you could cause another person to consider his or her relationship with Jesus. How cool is that?

Remember: we don't serve others so people will see us. We serve others so they'll see Christ.

Here's a practical idea for you: seek to serve everyone in your six-foot circle. In other words, wherever you go, imagine there is a six-foot circle around you. Who's in that circle? Does anyone in the circle need help? What can you do for them? Who could be encouraged or impacted because you took the time to care?

We look the most like Jesus when we are serving others.

¡ASPIRE TO KNOW MORE

▶ Want to know how good of a servant you are? See how you respond when someone treats you like a servant.

▶ Find Mark 10:45. Why did Jesus come to earth?

▶ Read Philippians 2:5–8. What are the things Jesus did in service to us?

iASPIRE TO CHOOSE FRIENDS WISELY

Do not let anyone fool you. Bad people can make
those who want to live good become bad.
1 CORINTHIANS 15:33

Friends are a great gift from God.

He certainly didn't owe us friendships in this life, but every true friend we have is a good gift from a gracious Father.

Here are two things to keep in mind about friends: First, friends will come and go. That isn't necessarily a reflection on you as much as it's a reality of life. Where you choose to live and what you choose to do will largely impact the people with whom you spend your time. Don't make bad decisions on big issues based on friends who may not even be part of your life in a few years. It's not worth it.

Second, your friends will have a bigger impact on you than you'll probably ever realize. Studies show that we become like the people we spend the most time with. Long-time married couples can actually start looking alike, sounding alike, and using similar handwriting. It's the way God designed us. We become like those we admire. So admire good people.

You'll never find a better friend than someone who points you to Jesus.

He who walks with wise men will be wise, but the
one who walks with fools will be destroyed.
PROVERBS 13:20

In Mark 2, the story is told of a paralyzed man who had four loyal friends. In fact, these friends decided their helpless buddy needed to see Jesus, so they picked up his bed and carried him to a house where Jesus was teaching.

Unfortunately, the crowd at the house was huge. There was no way they could get the paralyzed man inside. But these were good friends, and they made a plan. Just imagine this: the four guys climbed up the side of the house, removed part of the roof, and lowered their friend down in front of Jesus!

When Jesus saw the men's faith, He forgave the paralyzed man of his sin. Then Jesus healed the man of his condition and sent him walking home.

The paralyzed man had friends willing to get him to Christ at any cost. When you're choosing *your* closest friends—the people with whom you'll share your deepest thoughts and feelings—find people who will do anything to push you closer to Jesus.

If you go to a school or work at a job where most people don't know Jesus, look for someone who does. . .and aspire to help each other take a stand.

Do everything you can to have friends like the paralyzed man. Do everything you can to *be* that type of friend.

¡ASPIRE TO KNOW MORE

▶ Who do you know that loves God and would be a good friend? What can you do to reach out to that person and seek to build a better friendship?

▶ Find Proverbs 17:17. What can you expect from a true friend?

▶ According to Ephesians 4:32, what are three ways we can be a good friend?

38

¡ASPIRE TO BE GENTLE

Let all people see how gentle you are.
The Lord is coming again soon.
PHILIPPIANS 4:5

It's hard to be gentle with people who are wrong, isn't it?

Have you ever listened in frustration as someone described a movie or book and got all the details wrong? Or maybe someone tried to tell all about some subject that you clearly know more about. Even worse, have you ever been accused of doing something you didn't do?

Being gentle can be very hard, but that's what God wants from us.

Jesus knew more than anybody else, and He was treated less fairly than anyone, yet He chose to be gentle. He was gentle when He confronted the sinful woman at the well. He was gentle when He answered the baffled Nicodemus's questions. He was gentle when He invited children to sit on His lap and talk to Him. He was even gentle with His accusers. And He's been gentle with us even though we've sinned against Him countless times.

You may be thinking, *Hey, Jesus wasn't always gentle. What about that story of Him in the temple?*

In Mark 11, we see the city of Jerusalem packed with people observing the Passover, an important holiday in which the children of Israel remember what God did for them during their time in Egypt. Bible scholars estimate as many as *four hundred thousand* Jewish people were in town at the time. And, as often happens, moneymakers saw an opportunity in that crowd.

The temple would have been filled with activity as people came and went, worshiping God. They needed unblemished animals to offer in sacrifice, so merchants stepped up to provide them—at premium costs.

Entering the temple, Jesus saw the way people were being cheated in the name of worship, and He became angry. He turned over the merchants' tables and chairs, saying,

> *"Is it not written, 'My house is to be called*
> *a house of prayer for all the nations'?*
> *You have made it a place of robbers."*
> MARK 11:17

God wants us to be gentle with *people*, but He never commands us to be gentle with *sin*. Jesus knew the difference.

Every day, you have opportunities to interact with people. Often, they'll have different opinions than you do. Sometimes, they'll be difficult or frustrating or downright rude.

Be gentle.

If Jesus was never too good to be gentle with others, we must follow His example.

¡ASPIRE TO KNOW MORE

▶ Find Colossians 3:12. Since you are God's child, how should you live your new life?

▶ Read Galatians 6:10. According to this verse, we have a special responsibility to do good to whom?

iASPIRE TO DEFEND THE WEAK

*Do the right thing for the weak and those
without a father. Stand up for the rights of
those who are suffering and in need.*
PSALM 82:3

Have you ever felt bad because you weren't chosen for something? Maybe you tried out for a sports team or a school play and you weren't invited to participate. Maybe, in dodgeball, both team captains tried to push you to the other side.

Being left out, overlooked, or told you're not good enough is hard.

Here's some good news though. You don't have to wait to be picked by God. He chose you before the foundation of the world, and He loves you with an everlasting love.

*Even before the world was made, God chose us for
Himself because of His love. He planned that we
should be holy and without blame as He sees us.*
EPHESIANS 1:4

And belonging to God is more important than lining up with any other person or group.

Though God chose you and loves you deeply, He doesn't want you to get puffed up with pride. He doesn't want you to use that knowledge just to feel good about yourself. Instead, God wants you to look for others who are being left out or ignored—people who need to feel loved—and love them the way He loves you. (And, we might add, the way *He* loves them!)

Everybody deserves your attention, but there are specific groups of vulnerable people who God really wants you to watch out for. He wants you to care about widows and orphans. He wants you to care about unborn babies and little children. He wants you to care about people who are treated unkindly or unfairly because of what they look like or how they were made.

God wants you to care.

When the Bible tells us to defend the weak, the word *weak* isn't an indication of worth. Every person God makes is of infinite worth to Him. "Weak" simply refers to someone who is vulnerable because of life's circumstances. Anyone can be weak, in need of Jesus' love, at any time. And because of that, God wants us to love and defend them.

Keep an eye out for the weak. Do everything in your power to encourage and help them.

When Jesus commanded His followers to love like He loves, He knew the risk and the cost. He knew, for example, that He would die for people who could never repay Him. So when God tells *us* to love people, He wants us to do it expecting nothing in return.

Defending the weak is one way we love people the way Jesus loves us.

iASPIRE TO KNOW MORE

▶ Find James 1:27. In this verse, true religion is described in two ways. What are they?

▶ Think about the people in your life. Who is someone you can love and defend the way God loves and defends you?

40

¡ASPIRE TO HELP PEOPLE IN NEED

*Do not keep good from those who should
have it, when it is in your power to do it.*

PROVERBS 3:27

The world is filled with people in need. Our job is to help others whenever we can.

But it's important to understand *why* we help others. Because it feels good? So people will admire us for what we've done? So we'll be liked or respected?

No.

In fact, helping people doesn't guarantee any of that. Sometimes when we help people, we lose time, money, or respect. Sometimes our friends will laugh at us for being taken advantage of or for caring about someone who "doesn't deserve it."

Sometimes we get no thanks at all.

So why do it? *We help people in need because that is the Christlike thing to do.* And God will always help us.

*Let us go with complete trust to the throne of God.
We will receive His loving-kindness and have His
loving-favor to help us whenever we need it.*

HEBREWS 4:16

In Luke 10, Jesus told the story of a Jewish man who was traveling from Jerusalem to Jericho. On his journey, the man was attacked. Robbers beat him and stole all he had, leaving him half-dead at the side of the road. Before long, a priest came down the same road, saw the wounded man lying there, and did *nothing*. In fact, he passed by on the other side of the road. Soon after that, a Levite—a worker in the temple—came down the same road, and he too refused to help.

But then a Samaritan—a man from an ethnic group hated by Jews—appeared. When he saw the injured man, he decided to help. The Samaritan bandaged the Jewish man's wounds, put the man on his own donkey, and took him to an inn where he could get additional help. And then the Samaritan paid for all of it!

At the end of the story, Jesus asked, "Which of these three do you think was a neighbor to the man who was beaten by the robbers?" When an expert in the Jewish law answered, "The one who showed loving-pity on him," Jesus replied, "Go and do the same" (Luke 10:36-37).

We help people because God helps us in our need. Because He is so faithful to us, it is one of our great privileges to help others.

You know that kid nobody wants to sit with at lunch?

You know that older lady down the street who never leaves her house?

You know that teacher nobody likes?

What can you do today to help somebody in need?

¡ASPIRE TO KNOW MORE

▶ Read John 13:35. According to this verse, how will people know you belong to Jesus?

▶ What does Ephesians 4:28 say we're supposed to do instead of stealing?

▶ According to Hebrews 13:16, what is a gift you can give to God?

41

¡ASPIRE TO SHOW UP

Help each other in troubles and problems.
This is the kind of law Christ asks us to obey.
GALATIANS 6:2

Did you ever stop to think that friendship is a gift from God?

Throughout the Bible, we see several examples of good friends. Jonathan and David showed each other loyalty and sacrificial love. Elijah and Elisha served God together in ministry. Paul and Timothy worked together closely to spread the Gospel. Moses and Aaron (who were also brothers) teamed up to lead God's people out of captivity in Egypt.

In each case, the friends *showed up* in moments of need to help each other obey and please God. God gives us friendship in part so we can do more for Him. With the help of others, we can accomplish more than we ever would on our own.

In Matthew 11, the Pharisees accuse Jesus of being a friend of sinners. That was meant as an insult, but in reality, Jesus' friendship with sinners was (and is!) one of His greatest gifts. Because Jesus loves sinners, we can be made right with God.

Any good we accomplish is because Jesus is our friend.

So, do you consider your friendships here on earth to be a gift God has given to help you love and serve Him better? Or do you think of your friendships as just a way to have fun? God wants you to show up for your friends—to help them grow closer to Him. He also wants you to have the kind of friends who will show up in your time of need and help you become more like Jesus. That two-way street is what true friendship is all about.

Two are better than one, because they have good
pay for their work. For if one of them falls, the other

can help him up. But it is hard for the one who
falls when there is no one to lift him up.

Because God wants us to have friendships that point us to Christ, it's especially important that we spend the majority of our time with people who love God and want to serve Him. This doesn't mean we never spend time with unbelievers. And it certainly doesn't mean we should be unkind to anyone—in fact, it's just the opposite. The way we treat people can have a big impact on whether they want to know God.

But if we build our closest friendships with people who don't love God, they certainly won't help us become more like Jesus.

Let's aspire to build friendships for the glory of God.

¡ASPIRE TO KNOW MORE

▶ Read Hebrews 10:23–25. According to these verses, what should we help each other do?

▶ Find John 15:12–16. Is it possible for you to be the friend of Jesus? If so, how?

42

¡ASPIRE TO SPEAK UP

*"Have I not told you? Be strong and have strength
of heart! Do not be afraid or lose faith. For the Lord
your God is with you anywhere you go."*

JOSHUA 1:9

It takes courage to speak up.

Courage happens when we give our fears to God and choose to do and say the right things, no matter what.

In the Old Testament, Daniel was a Jewish teenager taken captive by Babylon to serve the king. Nebuchadnezzar worshipped idols and wanted everyone in Babylon to do the same, yet Daniel remained faithful to the one true God.

Eventually a new man, Darius, became king—and because Daniel was a hard worker with a good reputation, he was given a position of authority. In fact, the king planned to give Daniel power over the whole nation! Daniel's future looked bright. He would be rich and respected for the rest of his life.

However. . .

Evil men became jealous of Daniel's power, so they formed a nasty plan. They urged the king to create a new law that targeted Daniel, though that's not what they told Darius. All they said was "The king should make a law that must be obeyed, saying that anyone who asks something of any god or man besides you, O king, for thirty days, must be thrown to the lions" (Daniel 6:7). Foolishly, the king agreed.

If you were in Daniel's shoes, what would you do? Stop praying to God for a month? Surely He would understand, right? Just keep quiet until the storm blows over.

But Daniel had spent years honoring God with his life—and he wasn't going to stop now.

Even after the law was signed, Daniel continued praying three times a day, just as he had always done. In fact, he prayed *in front of his open window*, like he always did. He didn't even try to hide it!

You probably know the story. For breaking the law, Daniel was thrown into the den of lions, but something incredible happened. God protected him. And when King Darius got up early the next morning to check on his good, trustworthy official, Daniel gave God all the glory for keeping him safe. The lions hadn't touched him!

As a result, here's what King Darius said:

> *"I make a law that all those under my rule are to fear and shake before the God of Daniel. For He is the living God and He lives forever. His nation will never be destroyed and His rule will last forever. He saves and brings men out of danger, and shows His great power in heaven and on earth. And He has saved Daniel from the power of the lions."*
>
> DANIEL 6:26–27

You never know when your courage could change the course of history.

Be like Daniel. Aspire to speak up.

¡ASPIRE TO KNOW MORE

▶ Find Daniel 6. Read the full story of Daniel being thrown to the lions. (It's a story full of courage!)

▶ Speaking up can be hard at first, but it doesn't get easier until you do it. In other words, you learn to speak up *by speaking up*. How can you speak up this week?

¡ASPIRE TO TAKE GOOD RISKS

*"If anyone wants to keep his life safe, he will lose it.
If anyone gives up his life because of Me, he will save it."*

MATTHEW 16:25

God didn't create you to live a comfortable life. If that were His plan, He would have taken you straight to heaven as soon as you trusted Jesus as your Savior. Heaven, after all, will be the most comfortable place you could imagine!

Instead, God created you to glorify Him by doing important things for the sake of the Gospel. And some of those things could involve risk. For example, evangelism and missions are two of the best risks you could ever take.

Evangelism is simply sharing the Good News of Jesus Christ with other people. That can happen anywhere—at school, at home, at work, even at church. God is pleased when we share the love of Christ with others.

Missions is crossing culture to take the Gospel to people who don't yet know Jesus. Many people around the world have never even heard the Lord's name.

Right now, there are more than seventeen thousand people groups in the world. A "people group" is a collection of individuals who share things—such as language, location, or nationality—in common. Of those seventeen thousand people groups, more than seven thousand have yet to be reached with the Gospel. Overall, some *three billion people* still need to learn that Jesus loves them and died to save them. That's a job for us who already know Him:

*We are His work. He has made us to belong to Christ Jesus so
we can work for Him. He planned that we should do this.*

EPHESIANS 2:10

Have you ever dreamed of doing something big for God? Then start serving Him *today* in whatever ways you can. Love your neighbors, help your family, aid your church. Don't just watch other people worship—*participate*!

If you don't have a desire to serve God right where you are, you probably don't have the right motive to serve Him anywhere else.

But here's some exciting news: the teenage years aren't just a time for waiting around. God can (and has!) used teenagers throughout history to do big things for Him. He only requires that you love Him with your heart, soul, and mind—and that you commit yourself to obeying and following Him, no matter what.

Those risks are always worth taking!

---

iASPIRE TO KNOW MORE

▶ Find 1 Peter 2:9. What does God want you to do now that you belong to Him?

▶ Who around you needs to hear the good news of the Gospel? Can you call, visit, or write a letter and share what God has done in your life?

▶ With your parents' permission, go to www.joshuaproject.net and learn about some people groups around the world that still need to hear about Jesus.

iASPIRE TO DO HARD THINGS

So we can say for sure, "The Lord is my Helper.
I am not afraid of anything man can do to me."
HEBREWS 13:6

You can do hard things. Yes, *you.*

As human beings, we typically don't like to do hard things. We'd prefer the things that make us comfortable—things that require the least amount of effort and energy. But sometimes God calls us to do hard stuff for Him.

Sure, we enjoy the rewards that come with accomplishing big goals—running a marathon, earning good grades, setting a school record—but most of us don't enjoy the hard work it takes to get there. That's why students cheat on tests and athletes take illegal steroids. Many of us want the success without the sweat.

Or, as Jesus might say it, *the crown without the cross.*

Throughout the Bible though God tells us to do hard things: Deny yourself. Forgive your enemies. Bless those who curse you. Think of others as more important than yourself. Give what you have to those in need.

God isn't making life hard for you because He wants you to suffer. That isn't something a loving Father would do, and we know our God in heaven is a very, very good Father. So when He asks you to do something hard, it's because He knows it will be good for you. What brings Him glory is always good for you.

The Bible is filled with hard things we probably wouldn't choose for ourselves. But, thankfully, it also includes promises like this:

He is working in you. God is helping you obey Him.
God is doing what He wants done in you.
PHILIPPIANS 2:13

God will never ask you to do something without giving you the ability to obey. And He promises to be with you every step of the way.

So. . .are you willing to do the hard things that God wants you to do?

He may send you to a remote part of the world to share Jesus with people who have never heard the Gospel. On the other hand, He may call you to live with a difficult roommate or take a hard class at school or work in a job you don't like.

But He'll be with you. And doing hard things with God is better than doing easy things without Him.

The British author G. K. Chesterton once wrote, "The Christian ideal has not been tried and found wanting. It has been found difficult and left untried." It's true: the Christian life can be hard. But there is no better way to live.

¡ASPIRE TO KNOW MORE

▶ What hard thing does God want you to do? Ask Him for strength to do it for His glory. He'll help you.

▶ Find Genesis 22:1–19 to read about one of the hardest things God ever asked someone to do. How did God provide?

iASPIRE TO SHARE MY FAITH

Your heart should be holy and set apart for the Lord God.
Always be ready to tell everyone who asks you why you believe
as you do. Be gentle as you speak and show respect.

1 PETER 3:15

It takes courage to tell someone about Jesus.

It can be uncomfortable, because the Gospel tells every person that, until they accept salvation through Jesus, they have big problems. And people generally don't like being told there's something wrong with them. But for those of us who love Jesus, sharing our faith with others isn't just an option. It's both a command and a privilege.

Someone loved *you* enough to tell you the truth, right? Now you get to share with others:

"You are to go to all the world and preach
the Good News to every person."

MARK 16:15

But the possible rejection we face can feel scary or embarrassing. So how do we overcome our fear to tell people about Jesus?

Imagine knowing your neighbor's house was on fire and, even worse, that your neighbor was inside. If you cared at all about that person, you wouldn't casually call 9-1-1. Nor would you finish your math homework before deciding to get involved.

No—you'd get whatever help you could as quickly as possible. And you wouldn't care what people thought about *you* in the process. You'd only care about your neighbor's rescue.

A person's eternity—his or her relationship with God—is infinitely more important.

When we truly see people's need, we'll want to share the Gospel. We will be less concerned with our rejection, most concerned with their rescue. We will start conversations with people that ultimately lead to discussions of life and death. And we won't be embarrassed or angry if they reject us.

Whether a person knows God is the most important issue in life. It's even more important that a person knows God than it is for that person to escape a house fire, because an eternity apart from God will be far worse than a painful death on earth.

The good news for those of us who follow Jesus? We don't need to memorize some evangelism plan or learn a unique strategy. We simply need to care about people, to build friendships, and to invite others to consider their relationship with God. We don't lead people to Jesus—the Holy Spirit does. If we're faithful and obedient, we just get to be part of God's plan.

Does this mean sharing our faith is always easy? No, but it's always right.

When we truly understand what we have in Christ, we'll share Him with others.

¡ASPIRE TO KNOW MORE

▶ Who in your life right now needs to hear the Gospel? What can you do this week to start this important conversation?

▶ Find 2 Timothy 1:7. According to this verse, God did not give us the spirit of fear. What did He give us instead?

46

¡ASPIRE TO BE WELCOMING

Share what you have with Christian brothers who are in need.
Give meals and a place to stay to those who need it.

ROMANS 12:13

What do you think when you hear the word *welcome*? Do you think of inviting people into your house? Do you picture a sign on the front of a store, encouraging people to step inside to shop?

Inviting someone into your home or store is a good thing, but having a *life* that says "welcome" is even better.

What is a life that says welcome? It's an attitude that every person you meet has your attention, your help, and your compassion.

We should welcome others because our God is a welcoming God. Romans 15:7 says,

> *Receive each other as Christ*
> *received you. This will honor God.*

To welcome others the way God welcomes people is to love and serve *everyone*, not just the people we like the most. Jesus welcomed everyone, and so should we.

When the Lord lived on earth, He often upset the proud religious leaders by eating with the people who'd been rejected by society. Jesus cared about tax collectors and prostitutes, for example—people who were most disliked in Jesus' day. He ate with outcasts in order to share God's truth with them. He once explained it this way:

> *"When you have a supper, do not ask your friends or your*
> *brothers or your family or your rich neighbors. They will ask*
> *you to come to their place for a supper. That way you will be*

paid back for what you have done. When you have a supper,
ask poor people. Ask those who cannot walk and those who
are blind. You will be happy if you do this. They cannot pay
you back. You will get your pay when the people who
are right with God are raised from the dead."

LUKE 14:12–14

It's easy to be helpful to people who are helpful to us. But to those who don't deserve it? That's a totally different issue, right? It can be uncomfortable or even awkward.

But those are the people who need our welcome the most.

When we love the people who least "deserve" it, we're loving the way God loved us through Jesus. Once we know the love of God, it should completely change the way we love and welcome others.

"Dear friends, let us love each other, because love comes from God. Those who love are God's children and they know God" (1 John 4:7).

¡ASPIRE TO KNOW MORE

▶ You may not be old enough yet to invite people to dinner or to stay at your house, but what are some things you *can* do right now to have a life that says "welcome"?

▶ Find Matthew 9:9–13 to read about the time Jesus invited Matthew to be His disciple. According to these verses, what does God want instead of gifts to be given?

47

¡ASPIRE TO SEARCH FOR WISDOM

*How much better to get wisdom than gold! To get
understanding is to be chosen rather than silver.*
PROVERBS 16:16 ESV

By the time you graduate from high school—and especially by the time
you graduate from college—your head will be full of knowledge.

You'll know all kinds of things about math or English or music or art.
Maybe science or history will have been your favorite subjects, or maybe
you'll have learned something totally unique at your school.

Years of studying and doing homework will pay off because you'll
be full of information. But this information is just *knowledge*. What you
really need for a successful life is *wisdom*.

One of the most famous preachers in history, Charles Haddon
Spurgeon, said, "Wisdom is the right use of knowledge." In other words,
wisdom is *applying* the knowledge you have to the life you're living.

For example, you may be really good at math, but if you don't apply
that knowledge to paying your bills, it doesn't do you much good. Or
you might be great at memorizing Bible verses, but if you don't actually
apply the truth of those verses to the choices you make, what's the point?

When Solomon became king after his famous father, David, God
graciously invited him to ask for anything he wanted. Can you imagine?
What would you ask for—a car, popularity, perfect looks? There are so
many choices!

Solomon asked for *wisdom*. He knew he had a huge responsibility
to lead God's people correctly, and he wanted to please the Lord. And
how did God respond to this request?

*It pleased the Lord that Solomon had asked this. God
said to him, "You have asked this, and have not asked for a*

long life for yourself. You have not asked for riches, or for the life of those who hate you. But you have asked for understanding to know what is right. Because you have asked this, I have done what you said. See, I have given you a wise and understanding heart. No one has been like you before, and there will be no one like you in the future."

1 KINGS 3:10–12

To this day, King Solomon is considered the wisest king who ever lived.

Here's some good news: wisdom isn't just for those kids who make the best grades or have the highest IQs or get the most impressive test scores. Wisdom is for anyone who searches for it.

Just as God was pleased that Solomon wanted wisdom, He will be happy if you want wisdom too. In fact, God says He'll give His wisdom to anyone who asks for it.

Today is a good day to ask.

¡ASPIRE TO KNOW MORE

▶ Find James 1:5. If you find yourself in a tough situation and you need wisdom, what does God say will happen if you ask Him for it?

▶ Read James 3:17. According to this verse, what does wisdom look like?

48

¡ASPIRE TO BE WISE ONLINE

I will refuse to look at anything vile and vulgar. I hate all
who deal crookedly; I will have nothing to do with them.
PSALM 101:3 NLT

The internet can be a wonderful tool. We can listen to good music or send messages to missionaries overseas. We can learn lots of good information to help with our homework or school projects.

But if we're honest, we'll admit that the internet also provides many opportunities for us to make unhealthy, unhelpful, or unholy decisions. Whether it's watching video clips, looking at pictures, or browsing social media, we can easily forget that everything we do online either pleases or displeases God. Everything we choose to click makes us more or less like Jesus.

The apostle Paul had never heard of the Internet, but his words in Philippians 4:8 apply perfectly to our online experience:

Christian brothers, keep your minds thinking about
whatever is true, whatever is respected, whatever is right,
whatever is pure, whatever can be loved, and whatever
is well thought of. If there is anything good and worth
giving thanks for, think about these things.
PHILIPPIANS 4:8

Here are three simple pieces of advice to help you be wise online: First, *don't spend all your time on screens.* There's a whole world of opportunity away from the Internet. Go outside. Enjoy nature. Start conversations. Build in-person friendships. Help others. You won't regret the time you spend away from technology.

Second, *don't say anything online that you wouldn't say to someone in person.* If you wouldn't talk to strangers face-to-face, don't do it online, either. If you wouldn't say something rude or unkind to someone face-to-face, don't say something rude or unkind online, either. The internet can make us forget that we're talking to real people who need the love of Christ.

Third, *don't ever believe the lie that you can enjoy a little sin without it destroying you.* One of Satan's oldest lies is that you can get away with things God tells you not to do. This is the lie the devil fed Eve in the garden—the lie that ultimately plunged the world into sin and death. It's the same lie Satan will use to convince you that anything you want to do online is okay. Don't be fooled.

It breaks God's heart when we go to church and worship Him, then come home and find our entertainment through shows, websites, conversations, books, or jokes that make sin look good, funny, or enjoyable. Our sinful human nature automatically desires what is impure. Being entertained by things that make sin look good only feeds what we already want.

Being irresponsible online makes the essential fight against sin even harder. Aspire to be wise online.

¡ASPIRE TO KNOW MORE

▶ Find Proverbs 15:3. According to this verse, who sees every decision you make online?

▶ Read Philippians 4:8 again. Make a list of the things we're supposed to think about according to this verse. Is there anything you're currently doing online that you should stop? Ask God to help you.

iASPIRE TO HONOR MY PARENTS

"Honor your father and mother" (this is the
first commandment with a promise).
EPHESIANS 6:2 ESV

There will be days when your parents make mistakes. Your parents are human—just like you are—and all human beings make bad choices. It may seem to you like your parents don't acknowledge their mistakes, or it may feel like they make more wrong choices than they should. Regardless, Christian kids' responsibility is to honor their parents.

To "honor" means to show great respect, and throughout the Bible God tells us to honor our parents.

In fact, way back in the Old Testament, when God meets Moses on Mount Sinai to pass along the Ten Commandments, we see that the fifth rule on the list says,

"Honor your father and your mother, so your life may be
long in the land the Lord your God gives you."
EXODUS 20:12

Honoring your parents isn't just a good idea—it's a command from God.

So what are some ways you can honor your parents? How about praying for them? Showing appreciation. Helping them. Forgiving them.

As we get older, most of us realize that our parents were doing the best they could. Sure, they could have made different decisions along the way (and we can pray for grace not to make those same mistakes if God allows *us* to become parents). But no matter how we feel about Mom or Dad, God tells us to obey and honor our parents.

And He gives us an incentive:

Children, as Christians, obey your parents. This is the right thing to do. Respect your father and mother. This is the first Law given that had a promise. The promise is this: If you respect your father and mother, you will live a long time and your life will be full of many good things.

EPHESIANS 6:1–3

Notice that these verses don't say to obey your parents only when they're being kind and parenting correctly. They just say to obey and respect your parents so that life will go well for you.

One important note: God isn't saying that a person who dies young didn't honor his parents. We know this, for example, because Jesus was the most obedient son who ever lived. He honored His Father, and He died as a young man. But eternal life with God is certainly long. He sees and rewards what we do for *Him*.

God knows that your parents are going to make mistakes, and He's willing to use even those mistakes to make you more like Himself.

Your relationship with your parents is one of the most important ones you will ever have. When you honor your mom and dad, you're actually honoring God.

iASPIRE TO KNOW MORE

▶ What is something you can do to honor your parents today? Do you pray for your parents? If not, start today.

▶ Find Proverbs 6:20. This verse lists two ways you can honor your parents. What are they?

iASPIRE TO OBEY AUTHORITY

Children, obey your parents in
the Lord, for this is right.
EPHESIANS 6:1 ESV

Obedience isn't a feeling; it's a choice. And it's a choice God tells us to make.

In 1 Chronicles 13, King David decided to move the ark of the covenant—a special box that represented God's presence to His people—to Jerusalem. The journey would be about ten miles, so David had a new cart built in order to move the box.

God had some very important rules about this special box. For example, nobody except the chief priest was allowed to touch it, and that was only on special occasions. Everyone else was supposed to stand about three thousand feet away. These rules demonstrated God's holiness—His "set-apartness."

As David's men were moving the ark to Jerusalem, something terrible happened. The cattle pulling the wagon stumbled, and the special box started to slip off the cart. A man named Uzza put out his hand to stop the ark from falling, and when he touched it, Uzza died.

Wow.

But God demands obedience to authority. Even when we don't understand. Even when we don't feel like it. Even when we think we have a better idea.

Why does God tell us to obey the rules? Simply to make our lives more difficult? Because He doesn't want us to have fun? Because He doesn't really understand?

No. The answer is found in Hebrews 13:17:

Obey your leaders and do what they say. They keep watch over your souls. They have to tell God what they have done. They should have joy in this and not be sad. If they are sad, it is no help to you.

Your parents and everyone else who is responsible for you (including your pastors, teachers, and bosses) are accountable to God for how they lead you. They will answer to God for the choices they make.

And you are responsible to obey them. The only exception is that the authority is not asking you to disobey something God tells you to do in the Bible.

By now you probably know that your primary authorities in life—your parents—aren't perfect. They're going to make mistakes. But we trust that our parents have our best interests in mind even when they make decisions we don't like.

Obeying the authority in our lives is one of the best ways we obey God.

¡ASPIRE TO KNOW MORE

▶ Read Romans 13:1-2. Who puts people in charge?

▶ Find Colossians 3:20. What happens when you obey your parents?

▶ Look up John 14:23. According to this verse, if you love God, what will you do?

iASPIRE TO SEEK GOOD COUNSEL

Plans go wrong without talking together, but they will
go well when many wise men talk about what to do.
PROVERBS 15:22

Ever gone through an entire day and then discovered that your hair was sticking out in the back or you had something stuck in your teeth or your shirt was on backwards?

It's embarrassing! And it might leave you wondering why nobody told you.

We want to believe our friends will tell us the truth, don't we?

Finding people who are willing to be honest—especially about big things—is critically important in life. In reality, hair that sticks up or a shirt worn backwards isn't a big deal. But there are many more important issues in life that need good counsel from truthful friends.

Proverbs 27:6 says,

The pains given by a friend are faithful,
but the kisses of one who hates you are false.

According to this verse, it is better to have a friend who tells you the truth—even if it hurts—than to have a fake friend who only says nice things without meaning them. What's the point of having friends who give you bad counsel?

If you find a friend willing to be honest about the things that matter most, do everything you can to keep that friend close. If you have a friend, a parent, or a mentor who will tell you the truth for your good and growth, you have been given a gift.

So how do you know you've found someone who will give you good counsel? Answer: when you find a person whose advice and encouragement match what the Bible says. Biblical counsel is far better than words that make you happy or comfortable.

Good counsel doesn't just sound or feel good; it *is* good because it agrees with God.

Next time you need help making a decision, here are two good steps to take: First, *ask someone who is older than you for advice.* (And the older, the better!) If possible, ask several older people for advice and see if they agree. Proverbs 15:22 tells us there is safety in getting counsel from multiple people.

Second, *don't decide what you're going to do until* after *you ask for advice.* Sometimes we ask for advice, but we already know what we want to do. Asking with your mind made up isn't seeking good counsel; it's just looking for someone to agree with what you've already decided. Go into each conversation with an open mind to see what God would lead you to do.

A good counselor will give you advice that pleases God even if that advice isn't fun to hear. Far more important than telling you there's food stuck in your teeth is the input that leads you toward a wiser, more godly life.

Always seek good counsel.

---

iASPIRE TO KNOW MORE

▶ Find Proverbs 12:15. According to this verse, what do wise people do?

▶ Read Proverbs 13:10. According to this verse, who gets wisdom?

▶ Who is someone in your life that would make a good counselor?

52

¡ASPIRE TO SLOW DOWN

Be quiet and know that I am God. I will be honored
among the nations. I will be honored in the earth.

PSALM 46:10

We live in a high-speed world. Everything from our computer connections to our food service is *fast*. We can hop on a plane and be in another country by suppertime. We can email anyone in the world in the time it took our grandparents to address an envelope. We can buy things with the click of a button.

Our ancestors would truly be amazed at what we can do in the blink of an eye. But what has this high-speed pace of life taught us?

According to researchers, our culture struggles with impatience, worry, impulsivity, short attention spans, and lack of focus. We battle overactive minds and an inability to rest.

Basically, living at such a fast pace makes it harder to slow down and pay attention to spiritual things. But God's work in our lives rarely happens quickly. Growth is a slow process.

When we're young, it's hard to imagine wanting to slow down. School already feels like it will never end. We have lives to live, goals to reach, and milestones to achieve.

But God doesn't want you to rush through this season of life. He doesn't want you to miss the most important things while you're doing all the fast-paced stuff.

Luke 10 records the story of Jesus visiting His friends' home in a town called Bethany. And though the Bible doesn't say specifically, there could have been as many as a hundred people with Him that day, because everywhere Jesus went, crowds followed to hear Him speak.

When Jesus arrived at Mary and Martha's place, He began to teach.

Mary sat and listened to every word He said, but her sister was way too busy to sit. The Bible tells us that Martha was working hard to set supper ready. Can you imagine cooking for all those people—including Jesus—all by yourself? She probably felt a lot of pressure.

Martha finally got upset enough to speak out. She went to Jesus saying, "Do You see that my sister is not helping me? Tell her to help me" (Luke 10:40).

Martha was hoping Jesus would tell her sister to get busy, but He didn't. In fact, He commended Mary for her choice:

> "Martha, Martha, you are worried and troubled
> about many things. Only a few things are important,
> even just one. Mary has chosen the good thing.
> It will not be taken away from her."
>
> LUKE 10:41–42

Being busy and serving other people isn't a bad thing. In many other places, the Bible tells us to work hard and help others. But the most important thing for Martha (and for us) is to slow down, sit at Jesus' feet, and learn from Him.

You will never regret putting the brakes on your high-speed world to spend time with Jesus.

¡ASPIRE TO KNOW MORE

▶ Reread Psalm 46:10. What are some things you can do to quiet your life and spend more time with God?

▶ Find Matthew 11:28–30. Have you ever felt like you're carrying a heavy load? What is the solution?

53

¡ASPIRE TO LISTEN CAREFULLY

My son, listen to my words. Turn your ear to my sayings.
PROVERBS 4:20

You can learn a lot when you listen. For example, you can discover mistakes people have made that you can choose to avoid. You can learn what matters to people you care about so you can love them better. You can gain insights from teachers, pastors, and parents who are willing to invest time and truth into your life.

Listening is one of the most valuable skills you can learn. It can save you time, money, hurt, frustration, embarrassment, and regret. But it is a skill that takes determination and practice.

It isn't easy to truly listen. You have to empty your mind of other thoughts and to engage with the person who's speaking. But if you learn to do it well, you'll reap lifelong benefits.

The Bible is very clear about the importance of listening:

My Christian brothers, you know everyone should listen much and speak little. He should be slow to become angry.
JAMES 1:19

When you're learning to listen, the smartest thing you can do is *practice the pause.* In other words, when you're tempted to jump in and say something as someone else is talking, pause. Take a breath. Stay connected.

Proverbs 18:2 paints the picture of someone who is *not* good at listening:

*A fool does not find joy in understanding,
but only in letting his own mind be known.*

According to God's Word, we're foolish to be impatient with people or busy thinking about what we want to say next instead of truly listening. And chances are, if we're not good at listening to others, it's unlikely we're good at listening to God.

Truly paying attention to other people is one way we reflect our heavenly Father. The Bible tells us that God willingly and patiently listens to His children. If you are God's child and living right with Him, there is never a time when you call to Him—*day or night*—that He doesn't willingly listen to what you have to say. Isn't that incredible?

When Jesus walked on earth, He earned a reputation for lovingly listening to others, including children. Shouldn't we aspire to be like Him in this way?

What if we listened more and spoke less? How might life change for the better?

¡ASPIRE TO KNOW MORE

▶ Read 1 Samuel 3. What can we learn about listening from this story of young Samuel in the temple?

▶ What does Proverbs 18:13 say about someone who listens before he hears a matter?

▶ Today, *practice the pause.* Next time you're in a conversation, truly listen to what the other person is saying. When you're done, consider what new thing you've learned.

54

¡ASPIRE TO DENY DISTRACTION

Make the best use of your time.
These are sinful days.
EPHESIANS 5:16

One of Satan's go-to strategies for Christians is *distraction*. Distraction is anything that regularly takes your attention away from the most important priorities in your life. Distractions aren't necessarily bad things. They don't usually look sinful or feel destructive, which is why they can be so harmful. For example,

▶ Gamers spend about six hours each week playing.
▶ People spend about three hours every day on their phones.
▶ Teens spend about three hours a day on social media.

None of these things are evil by themselves. But if you spend three hours a day distracted by social media, that adds up to *forty-five days a year* that you could be doing more important things with your life.

And there are hundreds of ways to be distracted.

In Judges 13–16, we learn about an easily distracted man named Samson. He was a Nazirite, which means he had taken a special vow to serve God. Samson was given incredible physical strength from God to help protect his people from their enemies. He was so strong he killed a lion with his bare hands, and he killed an entire Philistine army using only the jawbone of a donkey. Samson had incredible potential.

Part of Samson's vow was a promise that he would not cut his hair. If he ever did, he would lose his strength. Samson knew this, and he protected his mane. He knew better than to share the secret of his strength with anybody.

But Samson got distracted.

Samson fell in love with a woman named Delilah. Nothing unusual about falling in love, but Delilah wasn't one of Samson's people. She didn't believe in the one true God, and she was in league with the Philistines, the sworn enemies of the Israelites.

Maybe Samson was distracted by Delilah's beauty, personality, or charm. Maybe he was just bored and looking for excitement. Whatever the case, the story didn't end well for this powerful warrior.

In Judges 16, Delilah tricked Samson into telling her the secret of his strength. Then she helped the Philistine leaders cut his hair. All of Samson's miraculous strength left him. He was captured, tortured, and forced to do hard work in a prison.

Samson's entire life changed for the worse when he got distracted from God's purpose.

We all run a similar risk if we allow ourselves to get distracted. Does this mean we can never do fun things? No, but it does mean we keep the main thing the main thing in our lives.

How should we respond to distraction? Pray like the psalmist:

> *Teach us to understand how many days we have.*
> *Then we will have a heart of wisdom to give You.*
>
> PSALM 90:12

Don't let distractions destroy you.

¡ASPIRE TO KNOW MORE

▶ Read Samson's whole story in Judges 13–16. Was he able to return to the Lord?

▶ What does Hebrews 11:32–34 say about Samson?

55

¡ASPIRE TO CONSIDER MY WORDS

Death and life are in the power of the tongue,
and those who love it will eat its fruit.
PROVERBS 18:21

Your words hold more power than you could ever imagine. Words can start wars, end lives, and ruin relationships. Words can also bring peace, save lives, and build relationships. *It's your choice.*

More than any previous generation, your words have impact. Why? Well, believe it or not, it wasn't that long ago that email, texting, and social media didn't even exist. A few decades ago, if you wanted to talk to someone, you had to visit, call, or send a letter. Today you can post a message that will be seen by virtually anybody in the world in the blink of an eye.

Your great-great grandparents would be astounded to know what you can do online.

So in an age when you can say anything to anybody at any time, aspire to consider your words carefully. It takes only seconds for your words to affect others—for good or ill.

When the Bible says that "death and life are in the power of the tongue," it isn't simply painting a word picture or exaggerating to make a point. Our words literally have the power to share eternal life—and, tragically, we have all heard how unkind words have caused some people to end their earthly lives. And, by the way, "the power of the tongue" goes beyond what we say out loud; it includes the words we post, email, or text.

Entertainers, politicians, and athletes have ruined their careers with a single sentence. Pastors have destroyed their ministries with a hurtful or hateful word. And God has warned against that for thousands of years:

There is one whose foolish words cut like a sword,
but the tongue of the wise brings healing.
PROVERBS 12:18

It's important to understand that the mouth speaks what fills the heart (Matthew 12:34). So if we want to speak words that bring life, we must start by evaluating what is already in our hearts. Hateful words come from hate in the heart. Kind words come from kindness in the heart.

It doesn't take more effort to be kind than it does to be mean. It isn't harder to be a friend than it is to be a bully. You don't need any more talent or intelligence than you have right now to be Christlike in what you say.

What you say matters. Aspire to make every word count.

¡ASPIRE TO KNOW MORE

▶ If you aspire to consider your words, find Psalm 141:3 and pray the verse to God.

▶ James 1:19 lists three ways we can make every word count. What are they?

▶ Read Ephesians 4:29. What does this verse tell us that our words can help others do?

iASPIRE TO STOP COMPLAINING

Be glad you can do the things you should be doing.
Do all things without arguing and talking about
how you wish you did not have to do them.

PHILIPPIANS 2:14

Have you had an X-ray? In some ways, an X-ray machine is like a high-powered camera that takes a picture of the inside of your body, particularly your bones. If you think you've broken your arm or leg, for example, the doctor may order an X-ray to find out, because the machine can see things that our eyes can't.

Complaining is like an X-ray machine. It shows us what is inside our hearts. Complaining is when we pour out our unhappy, frustrated, or envious thoughts and feelings. They either directly or indirectly question the goodness of God.

As Christians, most of us are wise enough not to openly say bad things about God. We probably won't speak the words *God is not good. God made a mistake. God doesn't keep His promises.*

But when we complain, we're saying some of these same things in an indirect way. If we think or say, "God didn't answer my request the way I wanted Him to," we really mean "God is not good." If we think, "I was born in the wrong family," we mean "God made a mistake." If we say, "God has forgotten about me," our heart is really complaining that God doesn't keep His promises.

What does the Bible say about complaining?

Watch your talk! No bad words should be coming
from your mouth. Say what is good. Your words
should help others grow as Christians.

EPHESIANS 4:29

Complaining isn't good. It doesn't help us or others grow in Christ. It always shows a lack of gratitude for what God has given.

Sure, school can be frustrating, but there are people who would do anything for the chance to get an education. Yes, family members can be hurtful, but there are people who would do anything to be part of a family. True, church can be disappointing, but there are people who would do anything to attend a service in total freedom. You realize that some people in other countries risk their lives to worship God, right?

Complaining, like an X-ray, is a picture of what we cannot see. Our grumbling shows us where harmful beliefs about God exist in our hearts. But with His help, we can correct our thinking and stop complaining today.

Truth: if God never gave us another good thing in our lifetime, He's already given us too much for us to complain.

¡ASPIRE TO KNOW MORE

▶ Is there anything in your life about which you need to stop complaining? If so, pause and ask God to help you. He will.

▶ Find 1 Thessalonians 5:16–18. According to these verses, what are the three things God gives us to do *instead* of complaining?

▶ In the Old Testament, the children of Israel were known for complaining. Read Numbers 11 to see what God thinks of that.

57

¡ASPIRE TO CHOOSE JOY

*Our hope comes from God. May He fill you with joy and
peace because of your trust in Him. May your hope
grow stronger by the power of the Holy Spirit.*

ROMANS 15:13

Joy isn't always linked to happy circumstances. It's a mistake, then, to believe *joy* and *happiness* are the same thing. Happiness usually comes from happy situations; joy doesn't depend on circumstances at all.

Sometimes we're so full of love and gratitude to God that it bubbles over into happiness in our hearts and on our faces. Praise God for those moments of pure happiness! The Bible never tells us *not* to be happy—happiness is another of God's gifts.

But joy is different. It doesn't come out as big laughs or wide smiles. Joy may tiptoe into your heart after you learn that someone you love has gone to be with Jesus or even after receiving a serious diagnosis or experiencing a devastating trial.

We can grieve losses on earth while rejoicing in the faithfulness of God.

Joy is a confident assurance—deeply rooted in our hearts—that God and His will are good, no matter what.

Jesus is the perfect example of someone who had joy even in hard times:

> *Looking to Jesus, the founder and perfecter of
> our faith, who for the joy that was set before Him
> endured the cross, despising the shame, and is
> seated at the right hand of the throne of God.*

HEBREWS 12:2 ESV

Because Jesus knows everything, He knew exactly what would happen to Him the night of His death. He knew about the utter pain and total rejection He would experience, yet—*for joy*—He endured the cross.

Jesus wasn't lighthearted about His crucifixion. We know this from His prayer in the garden where He asked God to spare Him from the cross (see Matthew 26:38–39). But He never lost sight of joy.

Joy is the defining mark—you could say "the logo"—of the Christian life. Talk to someone who loves Jesus deeply, and you'll talk to someone who is deeply joyful.

And the source of our joy is Jesus Himself. The reason for our joy is that we belong to Him.

Philippians is considered one of the most joy-filled books in the Bible. In just 104 verses, Paul uses the words *joy* or *rejoicing* sixteen times. Yet we know Paul wrote Philippians while he was in a dark, damp Roman prison waiting to see if he would live or die for his faith.

Paul was fully confident that God and His will were good.

We too can have that confidence, no matter what happens in life.

¡ASPIRE TO KNOW MORE

▶ Find Psalm 16:11 to see the secret of true and lasting joy. Where is joy found?

▶ Read Philippians 4:4. According to Paul (who was writing from a prison cell), how often should we be joyful?

58

¡ASPIRE TO BE KIND

You must be kind to each other. Think of the other
person. Forgive other people just as God forgave
you because of Christ's death on the cross.
EPHESIANS 4:32

One thing that must grieve the heart of God is how unkind people can be to each other.

Unkindness is everywhere—online, in schools, in churches, in homes. All you need to do is turn on the daily news to see examples of it. But unkindness is not God's desire. Here's what He wants us to do:

Love each other with genuine affection,
and take delight in honoring each other.
ROMANS 12:10 NLT

Because God made and loves every person on the planet, He cares deeply about the things we say and do to each other. He knows when we laugh at the way people look, talk, or speak. (And this must especially hurt God's heart since *He* made people exactly as they are!) God hears when we gossip and say mean things about our classmates at school. He sees when we're rude or disrespectful to people at church or home.

God knows, and He isn't pleased with unkindness *ever*. He wants us to love people the way He loves them. Remember, when Jesus walked on earth, He was kind to the people He met—even the ones who didn't like Him.

To the church in Colosse, the apostle Paul explained the difference between Christians and non-Christians, and he wrote these words to believers:

God has chosen you. You are holy and loved
by Him. Because of this, your new life should be full
of loving-pity. You should be kind to others and have
no pride. Be gentle and be willing to wait for others.

COLOSSIANS 3:12

When you're tempted to be unkind, remember how God wants you to treat people now that you belong to Him.

Research says that most people in the world struggle with these common fears: being rejected, being judged, being lonely, feeling worthless, feeling like a failure, feeling humiliated, being misunderstood, feeling unimportant, being unwanted, being disliked. The people you meet need the kindness of Christ, and you have a chance to provide that.

If there's any good news about all the unkindness in the world, it's this: when you are kind, it's so unusual that people know right away there's something different about you. You can use the opportunity to point people to Jesus.

But it also means that now—more than ever—children of God must *choose* to be kind. Let's aspire to treat everyone with grace.

¡ASPIRE TO KNOW MORE

▶ Read Romans 2:4. What are three examples of ways God has been kind to you?

▶ Find Luke 6:45. According to this verse, what does the mouth speak? And so—based on this verse—if we want to say kind things, what do we need to have in our hearts?

iASPIRE TO INTERCEDE FOR OTHERS

Be happy in your hope. Do not give up when trouble comes.
Do not let anything stop you from praying.
ROMANS 12:12

One of the greatest ways to be a true friend is to pray for those you love.

To *intercede* means to act on behalf of someone else. If you knew someone who was in trouble with the law and you wanted to help that person, you could go to a judge and plead for that person's freedom. In such a case, you would be *interceding*.

Here's another example: going to the Lord in prayer and pleading on another person's behalf. If you have a friend or family member who is going through something really hard, you plead with God to help that person you care so much about. You can even intercede for people you don't know, for example, for missionaries or Christian brothers and sisters who live in countries where they could be killed for following Jesus.

In the New Testament, the apostle Paul wrote to his friend Timothy,

First of all, I ask you to pray much for all men and to
give thanks for them. Pray for kings and all others who
are in power over us so we might live quiet God-like
lives in peace. It is good when you pray like this.
It pleases God Who is the One Who saves.
1 TIMOTHY 2:1-3

It pleased God that Timothy would pray for others—and it pleases God when *you* pray for others too. You don't even have to know or understand all the details, because God knows everything!

Of course, it's sometimes hard to remember to pray for other people.

We get busy living our own lives or praying for our own needs, and we can easily forget to intercede for others. Here are a couple of ideas to help you intercede: First, *choose a time that you can consistently pray for others*. If you have chores to do every day, use that work time for silent prayer. Pray for your friends while you unload the dishwasher or make your bed. Pray for missionaries while you take out the trash.

Second, *pray about a need as soon as you hear it*. Even though we may have the best intentions to pray for other people, we can easily forget to actually do it. As soon as you hear about a need, offer up a prayer, silent or spoken. And if you tell someone you'll pray about something, be absolutely sure you do it!

The greatest nineteenth-century evangelist D. L. Moody said, "Some people think God does not like to be troubled with our constant coming and asking. The way to trouble God is not to come at all."

You can never pray too much. Aspire to intercede.

¡ASPIRE TO KNOW MORE

▶ Find 1 John 5:14 to see the confidence you can have when you pray.

▶ Who can you pray for today? Stop and pray right now.

60

¡ASPIRE TO BE AN ENCOURAGER

*So comfort each other and make each
other strong as you are already doing.*
1 THESSALONIANS 5:11

Life is hard, and the world is full of reasons to be discouraged. Just check the news to see that people everywhere are suffering. The world is swamped with racial tension, political unrest, sickness, and death. Everywhere you look, someone is fighting somebody else. Bullies—both kids and adults—are everywhere.

Our world is full of pain. According to the apostle Paul, we're living in a world that's broken by sin, waiting for our Savior to come back and make all things right.

*We know that everything on the earth cries out
with pain the same as a woman giving birth to a
child. We also cry inside ourselves, even we who have
received the Holy Spirit. . . . We are waiting to become
His complete sons when our bodies are made free.
We were saved with this hope ahead of us. Now hope
means we are waiting for something we do not have.*
ROMANS 8:22-24

Everyone you encounter today needs hope.

So in a world that is broken and hurting, *aspire to be an encourager*. In a world that is filled with negativity, be the one who has something positive to say.

Hope is the most valuable thing you can offer somebody, and it costs you nothing to give. You can change someone's entire day by saying something encouraging.

According to Romans 15:5, our God is an encourager, and He wants us to spend our time encouraging others. Even your Bible was written as a form of encouragement.

> *For whatever was written in former days was written for*
> *our instruction, that through endurance and through the*
> *encouragement of the Scriptures we might have hope.*
> ROMANS 15:4 ESV

If you have hope in Christ, aspire to share your hope with others. That's one of the most profound ways to be a Christian in our current culture. *Wherever you are, be the person who is kind and encouraging to all.*

If you don't know where to start, just share a Bible verse with someone. You can give nothing greater than the promises of God. Hand someone a verse written on a card or send a verse in a text. Next time someone tells you about some hard, painful experience in his or her life, share something helpful that God has shown you in His Word. Offer to pray for people. . .and then do it! Listen carefully to what others say, and pray for wisdom to respond as Jesus would.

Being an encourager is easier and carries greater impact than you might imagine.

And get this: when you commit to encouraging others, something really wonderful happens. You realize *you* are being encouraged too.

iASPIRE TO KNOW MORE

▶ Find Proverbs 16:24. What are encouraging words like?

▶ Who can you encourage today? If you're nervous about it, start by picking someone you already know and love.

iASPIRE TO RESPOND CAREFULLY

*It will not go well for the man who hides his sins, but he who
tells his sins and turns from them will be given loving-pity.*
PROVERBS 28:13

Have you ever wondered why God called David a man after His heart even though David did some truly terrible things?

David's choices led to sexual impurity, murder, and the death of a baby. These are no small failures. It's safe to say David destroyed lives.

So why did God show him mercy? And even further, why did God honor David with the title "man after my own heart" (Acts 13:22 NLT)? Shouldn't a title like that be saved for someone who spent his entire life honoring God with his decisions?

The story of David's downfall is recorded in 2 Samuel 11. The chapter ends with the words "But what David had done was sinful in the eyes of the Lord" (v. 27). No question about it, David failed.

Months passed between the end of 2 Samuel 11 and the beginning of 2 Samuel 12. We know this because the baby David fathered in his sin was born during this time.

Nathan the prophet came to see David and told the king a parable—a simple story used to teach a big lesson. At the end of that story, Nathan told David that what he had done was wrong. In fact, the prophet said, "Why have you hated the Word of the Lord by doing what is bad in His eyes?" (2 Samuel 12:9).

Can you imagine hearing those words? None of us would ever say we "hate" God's Word, but sometimes our sinful actions say just the opposite.

David had multiple ways of responding to Nathan's accusation. He could have denied everything. He could have shouted, "I'm the king!" and had Nathan killed. He could have shrugged and said it didn't matter.

But here are the first words that came out of David's mouth:

"I have sinned against the Lord."
2 SAMUEL 12:13

Those six words may be the most important ones in the entire story of David. Because that was his response—because he repented and asked God to forgive him—the Lord took away David's sin and restored him completely.

God delights to forgive, but He requires our repentance.

Repenting of sin and asking forgiveness are hard things to do—especially today when "I'm sorry" has been replaced with "My bad," and true repentance gives way to blame shifting. But careful responses can be the difference-maker in anybody's story.

Next time you're caught in a sin (and we *all* sin), choose to be honest and humble. You'll never regret responding carefully.

¡ASPIRE TO KNOW MORE

▶ Which upsets you more—your mistakes and failures or the mistakes and failures of other people? Ask God to break your heart over your own sin so you can be right with Him.

▶ Find 2 Samuel 12:13. When David confessed his sin, how long did it take for God to forgive?

62

¡ASPIRE TO BE A PEACEMAKER

*Work for the things that make peace and help
each other become stronger Christians.*
ROMANS 14:19

Peace doesn't just happen. As humans, we naturally gravitate toward conflict and problems.

Need proof? Visit a classroom of toddlers, and see how long it takes for an argument to break out. Even before we can walk or talk, we want our own way.

But our Creator God values peacemaking. He knows our human nature—that we won't naturally pursue peace—and throughout scripture tells us many times and in many different ways to be peacemakers. Here's an example:

As much as you can, live in peace with all men.
ROMANS 12:18

Peace doesn't always depend on us. Sometimes we must have honest disagreements or speak up when we see injustice in the world. But as often as we can, we should pursue peace.

Here are three specific ways to be a peacemaker: First, *refuse to keep score*. "Keeping score" is when you keep track of what you've done for others versus what they've done for you—or when you keep track of who has done you wrong and what you plan to do to get even. Christ-followers who have been forgiven much by God have no right to keep score. God obliterated the scorecard of our sins against Him and replaced our enormous debt with His eternal compassion and forgiveness. We must follow His example.

Second, *learn to listen more and speak less*. That is James's New

Testament message: "My Christian brothers, you know everyone should listen much and speak little. He should be slow to become angry" (1:19). Many arguments are started, feelings hurt, and relationships ruined because we talk too soon, before we really *listen*. We think we understand what someone else is saying, then dive in to defend ourselves or lash out in anger. Even when you have something to say, *wait*.

Third, *choose to ask questions*. Sometimes, if we simply ask for clarification, we find that the misunderstanding is our own.

In a moment of anger or hurt, it can feel good to blurt out what we're feeling, but rarely does it turn out well. And very rarely does it glorify God. What helps?

A gentle answer turns away anger.
PROVERBS 15:1

No question about it, it takes humility to be a peacemaker. But Jesus was a peacemaker, and we should always aspire to be like Him.

¡ASPIRE TO KNOW MORE

▶ Find Matthew 5:9, part of Jesus' famous "sermon on the mount." What did He say results from being a peacemaker?

▶ Find Romans 16:20, 1 Thessalonians 5:23, and Hebrews 13:20. What do all three of these verses tell you about God?

▶ We can't be peacemakers until we have peace in our own heart. According to John 14:27, where does our peace come from?

63

¡ASPIRE TO TELL THE TRUTH

*Do not lie to each other. You have put
out of your life your old ways.*
COLOSSIANS 3:9

Telling the truth can be very hard. It can cost us our friendships or even our reputation. It can result in hurt feelings or other painful consequences. Sometimes, it's just easier to lie, isn't it?

But telling the truth is always the right decision.

God wants honesty. In fact, Proverbs 6:16-19 says God *hates* lying:

*There are six things which the Lord hates, yes, seven that are
hated by Him: A proud look, a lying tongue, and hands that kill
those who are without guilt, a heart that makes sinful plans,
feet that run fast to sin, a person who tells lies about someone
else, and one who starts fights among brothers.*

Did you notice that dishonesty appears twice in that list?

In the New Testament book of Acts, the story is told of a married couple named Ananias and Sapphira. They decided to sell a piece of their property, keeping some of the money for themselves and taking what was left to the church.

So far, so good. It's great to give back to God. He's pleased when we donate to church.

The problem came when Ananias and Sapphira decided to pretend they were giving *all* the money they had earned from selling their property. They wanted it to look like they were giving all they had. The couple may have believed the apostles would be impressed, or maybe they hoped everyone would think they were very generous people. Whatever their motive was, they lied.

After Ananias handed over the money, Peter said,

> *"Why did you let Satan fill your heart? He made you lie*
> *to the Holy Spirit. You kept back part of the money you got*
> *from your land. Was not the land yours before you sold it?*
> *After it was sold, you could have done what you wanted to*
> *do with the money. Why did you allow your heart to*
> *do this? You have lied to God, not to men."*
>
> ACTS 5:3–4

That must have been embarrassing. But the story doesn't end there. Acts 5:5 says, "When Ananias heard these words, he fell down dead."

Three hours later, Sapphira arrived, told the same lie, and died the same way.

God hates lying.

There are situations in which telling the truth could get you in trouble because you're admitting to doing something wrong. At other times, telling the truth could mean you won't be as popular as you'd like, because you're standing up for what's right. Either way, it is always God's will for you to be honest.

Lying inevitably ends up costing more than you want to pay. Aspire to tell the truth.

¡ASPIRE TO KNOW MORE

▶ Read Ephesians 4:17–32. These verses talk about what should change when a person follows Christ. What, specifically, does verse 25 say should change?

▶ Read Matthew 26:69–75 to see how Peter himself once lied—and what the result was. Then find John 21:15–19 to see how Jesus forgave Peter.

64

¡ASPIRE TO LOVE GOD MOST

But as it is written, Eye hath not seen, nor ear heard,
neither have entered into the heart of man, the things
which God hath prepared for them that love him.

1 CORINTHIANS 2:9 KJV

Throughout the New Testament, many people followed Jesus. Some were sincere, following out of love and a desire to be like Him. Others, though, followed Jesus because they wanted things *from* Him. Some followed Jesus for the excitement of His miracles. Others might even have followed Jesus to see the fireworks when He rebuked the arrogant religious leaders.

So in every city, as Jesus did His thing, the crowds grew bigger.

But then an interesting thing would happen.

To the huge crowds following Him, Jesus would give what the Bible calls "a hard saying" (John 6:60 KJV). In other words, He would teach the crowds a truth that just didn't feel good, and the crowds would dwindle to just those who truly loved Jesus for the right reasons.

For example, Jesus once told the crowds that they couldn't be His disciples if they didn't "hate" their fathers, mothers, spouses, children, and siblings (Luke 14:26). *Huh?*

Obviously, Jesus wasn't telling people to hate their own family members. That would contradict other things He had said. But He was saying that we should love God so much that our love for everything else pales by comparison. He was saying we should choose to love God most. Here's another way He said that:

> *"He who loves his father and mother more than Me*
> *is not good enough for Me. He who loves son or*
> *daughter more than Me is not good enough for Me."*

MATTHEW 10:37

It's never been a popular message, but it's an important one: you cannot love more than one thing or person *the most*. Either you love God most, or you love something or someone else more. And loving anything more than God is sin.

We should love God so much that our love for Him controls everything we think and do. As the psalm writer wrote,

> O God, You are my God. I will look for You with all my heart
> and strength. My soul is thirsty for You. My flesh is weak want-
> ing You in a dry and tired land where there is no water.
>
> PSALM 63:1

If we love the things God gives more than God Himself, we will never find satisfaction in this life. But if we love God with our heart, soul, and mind, using the gifts He gives to glorify Him, then we will always find that He is all we need.

¡ASPIRE TO KNOW MORE

▶ Find Mark 12:29–30. What does the Bible say is the most important commandment?

▶ Read Deuteronomy 7:9. With whom does this verse say God keeps His promises?

▶ Look up Romans 8:28. For whom does God work all things together for good?

65

¡ASPIRE TO TRUST GOD COMPLETELY

*Trust in the Lord with all your heart, and do
not trust in your own understanding.*

PROVERBS 3:5

When God promises something in His Word, we honor Him by believing what He said—even if it doesn't feel good. Even when it doesn't make sense.

Life is hard. If it hasn't already happened, there will come a day when you will be absolutely crushed by something that did not go according to your plan. It will hurt a lot. And you'll wonder if God has forgotten you or if maybe you're paying for some sin you committed in the past. You may wonder if you can keep going. You may beg God to fix things and make you feel better.

In those times, when you can't sleep and your mind is racing to unhelpful thoughts, remind yourself of these truths:

> *God is for you not against you* (Romans 8:31).
> *God will give you everything you need* (Philippians 4:19).
> *God will make everything in your life work together for good* (Romans 8:28).

See, everything in your life (everything in the whole world, really) will eventually change. Life itself is a vapor, a mist that is here and gone in the blink of an eye. Because you're young, it may not feel that way right now. Right now, it probably seems like adulthood is a lifetime away. But one day you'll realize that twenty or thirty or forty years have passed much faster than you thought possible.

Everything changes. Everything but God. He is the only unchanging reality—yesterday, today, and forever. Your biggest job in life is to trust Him even when things don't make sense. Maybe more to the point, *especially* when things don't make sense.

Here is one of the great truths about God: He doesn't make choices based on feelings or whims or moods. His holiness hinges on His truthfulness to the promises He's made. And He will keep every single one.

Because God is good and only does good, we can be sure His plans are greater than our plans every single time. This doesn't mean life will never hurt. It absolutely will hurt at times, but we have the assurance that God loves us and has our good in mind.

If you have a question for God, *ask Him*. If you are confused, hurt, frustrated, or discouraged, *tell Him*. And then after you do, *trust Him*.

We can trust that the story He is writing for us is a good one.

¡ASPIRE TO KNOW MORE

▶ Find 1 Peter 1:8–9. What will you receive if you trust God completely?

▶ Look up Job 42:2, the end of an amazing story of human suffering. How did Job respond to God?

▶ What do you need to trust God with today? Pray and talk to Him about it.

66

¡ASPIRE TO DEFEAT FEAR

*For God did not give us a spirit of fear. He gave us
a spirit of power and of love and of a good mind.*
2 TIMOTHY 1:7

Anxiety never tells the truth. It's a liar, and it isn't working for your best
or God's glory.

When we're anxious, we're likely imagining a scenario in which God
isn't present or able to defend us. Yet God's children *know* He's committed
to be with them at all times.

So the way we defeat fear isn't by being less afraid; we defeat fear
by *trusting God more.*

Don't tell yourself, "I will never be afraid." That's impossible for human
beings. Instead, say with the psalmist,

When I am afraid, I will trust in You.
PSALM 56:3

Fearful thoughts, we can be sure, aren't from God. He doesn't want
us to be afraid. In fact, hundreds of times in the Bible, God tells us not
to be afraid. He uses phrases such as "Fear not," "Do not be afraid," "Do
not be dismayed," "Be anxious for nothing," and "Do not fear."

Notice that these are commands. We must *choose* to trust God,
believing that if something hard or scary happens in the future, He will
be there to walk through it with us. God won't leave us to face fearful
situations by ourselves. And He will meet every one of our needs.

Through the prophet Isaiah, God gave us a glimpse into His perfect
care for His children:

*"Do not fear, for I am with you. Do not be afraid,
for I am your God. I will give you strength, and for*

sure I will help you. Yes, I will hold you up with
My right hand that is right and good."
ISAIAH 41:10

So we trust God by believing His promises—every single one of them.

God's promises must be bigger to us than our worst "what if?" questions. Every day we should choose to make what we know about God bigger and better than what we don't know about the future.

The battle to defeat fear is primarily a battle of the mind. When scary situations arise, we ask ourselves two questions:

1. Do I believe what God has promised me in His Word?
2. Do I trust that His plans for me are good?

If the answer to either of those questions is no, we'll be fearful every time. But if we trust Him, we'll discover that "the peace of God is much greater than the human mind can understand. This peace will keep your hearts and minds through Christ Jesus" (Philippians 4:7).

Defeating fear only comes as we increase our faith and trust in God.

¡ASPIRE TO KNOW MORE

▶ Find Matthew 10:28. Who is the only one we should fear?

▶ Look up the word *antidote* in a dictionary. Then look up 1 John 4:18. According to this verse, what is the antidote to fear?

▶ Copy Psalm 46:1 and put it in a place where you can read it when you are afraid.

67

¡ASPIRE TO WORRY LESS

*Give all your worries to Him
because He cares for you.*
1 PETER 5:7

Worry is one of the most acceptable sins, isn't it?

We'd be shocked to hear someone say, "I really want to steal something today!" It would be very strange if someone said out loud, "Man, I just want to worship another god." And yet people say "I'm worried" all the time—and it seems like no big deal.

But worry *is* a big deal because it reflects our heart's distrust in God. What we're saying when we worry is that we don't think God can handle our situation.

Sure, God was powerful enough to create the universe. . .*but can He really help me on my English test*? God loves us enough to save us from hell. . .*but can He really help me repair a broken relationship*?

It's silly when we put it that way, isn't it? But that is what we do when we worry.

Worry is a shift in trust. When we worry, we stop trusting what God has promised and start trusting what we think.

The problem is nothing new. In fact, when Jesus walked the earth, He talked to His followers about worry, which means they must have struggled with it too.

*"I say to you, do not worry about your life, what you are
going to eat. Do not worry about your body, what you are
going to wear. Life is worth more than food. The body is worth
more than clothes. Look at the birds. They do not plant seeds.
They do not gather grain. They have no grain buildings for*

keeping grain. Yet God feeds them. Are you
not worth more than the birds?"
LUKE 12:22–24

Answer: *Of course* Jesus' followers were worth more than birds! And so are you.

Since worry is a natural, human response, we must aspire to defeat our fears by believing big truths about God. One practical way we fight worry is with gratitude. Throughout the Bible, God links *not being worried* with *being thankful*, for example,

Do not worry. Learn to pray about everything.
Give thanks to God as you ask Him for what you need.
PHILIPPIANS 4:6

If you want to stop worrying, start being more thankful to God. Acknowledge what He's doing for you now and what He will do for you in the future. And then trust Him to keep His Word.

God never abandons His creation, especially those for whom Jesus died.

¡ASPIRE TO KNOW MORE

▶ Spend a day listening to how often you—or people around you—use the word *worry*. Is worry something you need to work on? If so, ask God for help.

▶ Read Matthew 6:28–29. What big truths about God in these verses will help us fight worry?

▶ Find Psalm 118:6. According to this verse, what is the greatest reason we have not to worry?

68

¡ASPIRE TO LOVE LIFE

You will show me the way of life. Being with You is to be
full of joy. In Your right hand there is happiness forever.
PSALM 16:11

What happens if you don't get to live the life you've dreamed of?

It's good to have dreams and aspirations. It's good to imagine growing up, getting married, and serving God. There's no harm in envisioning all the wonderful things God can do with our lives on earth.

But sometimes God has different plans for us. Sometimes our lives end up far from what we'd imagined, and this can result in deep disappointment.

Some people dream of getting married but never do. Some people want children but can't have any. Some people envision earning scholarships, playing major league sports, or joining the military but never get the opportunity.

When our dreams are crushed, we may be tempted to ask questions like "What did I do wrong?" "Does God care about the desires of my heart?" "What happened to the life I dreamed of living?"

God *does* care about you and your life. In fact, He cares so much that He won't give you what you want if it isn't what He knows is best. In the Old Testament, the prophet Jeremiah delivered these words to exiles in Babylon who weren't living the lives they imagined:

"For I know the plans I have for you," says the Lord,
"plans for well-being and not for trouble,
to give you a future and a hope."
JEREMIAH 29:11

When life doesn't go as planned, we must deliberately choose to take our eyes off our disappointment and fix our gaze on God. He deserves our full trust. He knows what's best, and He's following a plan for our lives that's far better than anything we could create for ourselves.

It's okay to feel sad about dreams that don't come true. It's okay to ask God good, hard questions. It's even okay to pour out your heart to Him. But after you've done those things, it's important to love the life God has given you. Here's what another Old Testament prophet, Isaiah, said:

> *"Do not remember the things that have happened*
> *before. Do not think about the things of the past.*
> *See, I will do a new thing. It will begin happening now.*
> *Will you not know about it? I will even make a road*
> *in the wilderness, and rivers in the desert."*
> ISAIAH 43:18–19

God is good at making roads in the wilderness. Just wait and see what He can do.

¡ASPIRE TO KNOW MORE

▶ Read Jeremiah 29:10–14. How long would the Israelites be exiles in Babylon before God kept His promise to bring them back? God doesn't always move quickly, but He always keeps His word.

▶ What has disappointed you in life that you need to trust God to handle? Pray and ask Him for the strength to trust and obey.

69

¡ASPIRE TO THINK ABOUT DEATH

*Our human bodies made from dust must be changed into
a body that cannot be destroyed. Our human bodies that
can die must be changed into bodies that will never die.*

1 CORINTHIANS 15:53

Death isn't typically a topic we enjoy. Understandably, it can be very uncomfortable. We have many unanswered questions, don't we? The process of death is largely unknown until we experience it, so our culture goes to great lengths to avoid thinking about it.

But did you know God *wants* us to think about death?

No, He doesn't want us to sit around in morbid thoughts, nor does He ever want us to be afraid of death. If we know Jesus as Savior, we have nothing to fear when we die.

> *O death, where is your power? O death, where
> are your pains? The pain in death is sin. Sin has
> power over those under the Law. But God is the
> One Who gives us power over sin through Jesus
> Christ our Lord. We give thanks to Him for this.*

1 CORINTHIANS 15:55–57

So why would God want us to think about death?

He wants us to remember that there is much more to life than simply our time on this earth. In fact, because life is short and eternity forever, we have far more to look forward to *after* death than we do right now. But death also means we'll stand face-to-face before the Lord, and we should do all we can in this life to be ready for that moment.

Nothing will ever be more important than that second you stand before Jesus when you die. So living this life like death isn't coming (or doesn't matter) would be a terrible mistake.

Throughout the Bible we learn that wise people think about death, but fools ignore the topic. The wise allow death and eternity to impact the way they live, but the foolish will live like this life is all that matters.

Solomon—the wisest man who ever lived—said it this way:

> *To have sorrow is better than to laugh because when*
> *a face is sad, the heart may become strong. The*
> *heart of the wise is in the house of sorrow, while the*
> *heart of fools is in the house where there is fun.*
> ECCLESIASTES 7:3-4

In other words, it's better to attend a funeral than a party.

Huh? Most of us would much rather attend the party. But Solomon understood that funerals cause us to think about death and eternity. Parties only get us thinking about life and having fun.

Aspire to think about death. It'll change the way you live.

¡ASPIRE TO KNOW MORE

▶ Read Philippians 1:21. This verse gives us the reason we should have no fear of death or dying if we know Christ.

▶ Find 2 Corinthians 4:16-18. According to these verses, what are the little troubles in life preparing us for?

iASPIRE TO GRIEVE DIFFERENTLY

The Lord is near to those who have a broken heart.
And He saves those who are broken in spirit.

PSALM 34:18

In a matter of minutes, entire lives can be turned upside down. We can get a hard phone call, or we can receive bad news from someone at the front door. We can read a painful text message, or we can receive a scary medical diagnosis.

And all of these things can rightfully result in grief.

Grief is an emotional response to loss.

As a follower of Jesus, you are never told to stuff your pain or act like tough things don't hurt. The Bible never commands you not to cry.

In John 11, we read about two sisters—Mary and Martha—and their brother, Lazarus. Lazarus is sick, and his sisters send word to Jesus, asking Him to come and heal His friend. Mary and Martha know that Jesus has the power to make everything okay.

But Jesus doesn't come right away. Lazarus dies.

Understandably, the Lord's delay confuses Mary and Martha, and by the time Jesus does arrive, Mary falls at His feet and says, "If You had been here, he wouldn't have died."

Watching Mary and Martha grieve the loss of their brother, Jesus could have responded in several ways. He could have walked away and done nothing more. He could have rebuked them for not trusting Him. He could have told them to stop crying because He knew what would happen next. But instead, Jesus did something we might not expect the Son of God to do:

Jesus cried.

JOHN 11:35

John 11:35 is the shortest verse in many translations of the Bible. But it is also one of the most powerful. Jesus wept not because He lacked faith in God but because His friend had died. John 11:33 tells us that Jesus saw Mary crying, and "His heart was very sad and He was troubled."

Jesus demonstrated that grief is a natural response to pain and loss.

Thankfully, the Bible never tells us not to grieve. It simply tells us to grieve *differently* than people who don't know Jesus. Why?

> *You have no reason to have*
> *sorrow as those who have no hope.*
> 1 THESSALONIANS 4:13

No matter what you experience in your life, if you know Jesus, *you are not hopeless.*

You may *feel* hopeless. Your circumstances may *look* hopeless. But you are *not* hopeless, *ever.*

God never promised that life for His children would be easy. In fact, just the opposite. The Bible tells us that life in a fallen, broken world will be full of heartache and trouble, but God promises to be with us every step of the way.

Grieve when hard things happen, but grieve with hope.

¡ASPIRE TO KNOW MORE

▶ Read John 11:1–44. What ended up happening to Lazarus?

▶ Do you believe Jesus knew what would happen to Lazarus even before He wept with Mary? (Hint: Jesus is omniscient. Look up *omniscient* in the dictionary if you don't know what it means.)

iASPIRE TO THINK ABOUT HEAVEN

Keep your minds thinking about things in heaven.
Do not think about things on the earth.
COLOSSIANS 3:2

You were made for heaven and fellowship with God.

When we're young, it's hard to think about heaven. Unless Jesus comes back first, we'll have to *die* to get there. And we typically don't want to think about death when we have life to live!

But God wants us to think about heaven because *He* is there. And being with Him is the thing that matters most.

> *But we are citizens of heaven. Christ, the One Who*
> *saves from the punishment of sin, will be coming down*
> *from heaven again. We are waiting for Him to return.*
> PHILIPPIANS 3:20

If we're truly citizens of heaven, we should be *thinking* about it. We should be *planning* for it. We should be *living* for it. Certainly, if we're citizens of heaven, what happens in heaven should be at least as important, if not more so, as what happens to us here.

Being a citizen of heaven should change the way we live on earth.

It's natural to crave satisfaction—we're wired for that. The Bible says our only true satisfaction comes from loving and serving God with our heart, soul, and mind. Nothing less than living for Him will satisfy you—not a nice house, not a new car, not a good job, not a fun relationship. God made you to crave relationship with Him, and anything less than that will leave you wanting something more.

So live with eternity as your motive for all you do. Here's how Jesus put it:

"Do not gather together for yourself riches of this earth. They will be eaten by bugs and become rusted. Men can break in and steal them. Gather together riches in heaven where they will not be eaten by bugs or become rusted. Men cannot break in and steal them. For wherever your riches are, your heart will be there also."

MATTHEW 6:19–21

God tells us to gather riches in heaven instead of on earth because He wants us to live a heaven-centered life. What does that look like? Sharing the Gospel with people you meet and especially those you know and love. Placing a higher priority on serving God than on collecting nice things. Not fearing the future because God is there.

When you read the history of faithful men and women who made an impact on this world for God's glory, what you'll always discover is that they lived with heaven in mind. Aspire to do the same.

iASPIRE TO KNOW MORE

▶ Find 1 Timothy 6:7. What do you get to take with you when you die? How should this change the way you live?

▶ Want a glimpse of heaven? Read Revelation 5:11–14.

▶ What can you do today that will count for eternity?

iASPIRE TO WAIT PATIENTLY

But they who wait upon the Lord will get new strength.
They will rise up with wings like eagles. They will run and
not get tired. They will walk and not become weak.

ISAIAH 40:31

Waiting can feel like you're doing nothing, can't it? But waiting is actually hard work.

When we're waiting patiently for God to do something for us—to help us finish a long school year, make new friends, discover His plans for our future, receive the answer to a prayer request—we're actually doing the opposite of nothing.

Waiting patiently requires us to do things like trust, rest, pray, obey, listen, and hope.

Psalm 37:7 is an interesting verse about waiting. It says,

> *Rest in the Lord and be willing to wait for Him.*
> *Do not trouble yourself when all goes well with*
> *the one who carries out his sinful plans.*

The beginning of that verse is easy to understand: "Rest in the Lord and be willing to wait for Him." All good, right? Even if it's hard to do, we know what it means to rest and willingly wait for God. But the verse doesn't end there.

The second part of Psalm 37:7 says, "Do not trouble yourself when all goes well with the one who carries out his sinful plans."

When we're waiting for God to answer a prayer or help us with a problem or provide for a need, it's human nature to look around and see what He's doing for other people. And it's especially tempting to check what's happening in the lives of people who don't love or serve God the way *we* think they should.

Why did God let that guy win the contest? We all know he's mean.

Why is God giving her so many friends? We all know she's fake.

Why did God put them in a family with lots of money? We all know they're not grateful.

It's hard to be patient when we feel like we're being left out. But God commands us to wait patiently, and He gives us good reasons to do so.

First, we must trust that God's thoughts are not our thoughts and His ways are not our ways (Isaiah 55:8). He knows infinitely more than we do about what every person needs. (*Infinitely*, by the way, just indicates "without limit.") If God blesses another person with something *you* want, He knows that person needs it more than you do.

Second, we must believe our big God is able to do big things. Our waiting isn't just wasting time; it's about learning to trust God completely.

Until God's perfect time arrives (and only He knows when that is), nothing you do or say will make something happen. When it *is* God's time, nothing you do can stop His perfect will.

¡ASPIRE TO KNOW MORE

▶ What are you waiting on God for right now? Find Psalm 25:5 and pray those words to God.

▶ Read Titus 2:13. What is the greatest thing we should be waiting for every day of our lives?

iASPIRE TO LET GO OF HURTS

*After you have suffered for awhile, God Himself will make you
perfect. He will keep you in the right way. He will give you strength.
He is the God of all loving-favor and has called you through
Christ Jesus to share His shining-greatness forever.*

1 PETER 5:10

Is there someone in your life you need to forgive? Or a past hurt that you're hanging on to? Why not make today the day you give your pain and disappointment to God?

Maybe somebody did something really awful to you. Maybe something totally unfair happened in your life. Maybe you've been waiting a long time for an apology that you haven't received. (And maybe you'll go your entire life without getting the apology you deserve!)

Whatever the case, God wants you to let go of your hurts. Specifically, He wants you to give your disappointments—*all of them*—to Him. Then He tells you to trust Him to take care of whatever or whoever has hurt you.

What does God do when we give our broken heart and hurt feelings to Him?

*He heals those who have a broken
heart. He heals their sorrows.*

PSALM 147:3

Another translation says God "binds up their wounds," which sounds like something a doctor would do, doesn't it? God is the Great Physician, and He can fix your broken heart. But you have to go to Him and trust Him to do the work. A patient doesn't tell the physician how to do his job, nor does he guide a doctor during the surgery. The patient rests and trusts that the physician knows what he's doing.

It's easy (and very natural) to hold on to grudges, but that's not God's desire. Hanging on to hurts only hurts *you*. Here's what God tells you to do instead:

> *Put out of your life all these things: bad feelings about other people, anger, temper, loud talk, bad talk which hurts other people, and bad feelings which hurt other people. You must be kind to each other. Think of the other person. Forgive other people just as God forgave you because of Christ's death on the cross.*
> EPHESIANS 4:31-32

Guess what? There's a day coming when God is going to make everything right. You can't help whether you're treated correctly, but you can choose to trust God when you're *not* treated correctly. God sees, God knows, and God cares.

In fact, He wants you to let go of hurts so He can give you something better. It may be a new friendship or a new opportunity—maybe something far better than anything you've lost—but no matter what He has planned for your future, you will have a closer walk with Him.

God is *always* better than any hurts you're hanging on to. Aspire to let them go.

¡ASPIRE TO KNOW MORE

▶ Are you hanging on to a hurt today? Pray and give it to God. And if you need to give to God again, do that as often as necessary.

▶ Find Psalm 34:18. Where is God when you are hurting?

74

¡ASPIRE TO FORGIVE AS JESUS DID

*You must be kind to each other. Think of the other
person. Forgive other people just as God forgave
you because of Christ's death on the cross.*
EPHESIANS 4:32

Life is filled with relationships. They add so much to our days, but in a fallen world, those relationships can get broken.

We hurt each other—both accidentally and intentionally—and what we do with those hurts determines how we live. Forgiving (or not forgiving) makes all the difference.

When we've been hurt, we form an invisible link with the person and offense that gave us pain. We think about them, talk about them, worry about them. The only way to cut the invisible cord and live in the freedom God desires for us is by offering forgiveness.

*Try to understand other people. Forgive each other.
If you have something against someone, forgive him.
That is the way the Lord forgave you.*
COLOSSIANS 3:13

But let's be honest, even though we know forgiveness is a good idea, it sometimes feels impossible.

Would God really ask me to forgive if He understood how badly I was hurt?

The truth is, He does understand how bad people's offenses make us feel. He has forgiven far more from us than we will ever need to forgive anyone else. And He wants us to forgive for our good and His glory.

So how does it look to forgive like Jesus did? Here's how the apostle Paul described it:

Never pay back someone for the bad he has done to you.
Let the anger of God take care of the other person. The Holy
Writings say. . . "If the one who hates you is hungry, feed him.
If he is thirsty, give him water. If you do that, you will be
making him more ashamed of himself." Do not let sin have
power over you. Let good have power over sin!

ROMANS 12:19–21

Here is an easy way to know whether you're forgiving as Jesus does: When you think of the wrong you've experienced, what do you think about next? God's promise to take care of it or your enemy's responsibility to pay?

The answer tells you everything you need to know.

Forgiveness isn't about letting someone off the hook—it's about trusting God. It's about treating others the way you want God to treat you when you sin against Him.

When we forget the forgiveness we've received from God, we fail to give this same forgiveness to others.

It's hard but necessary: forgive, forgive, *forgive.*

¡ASPIRE TO KNOW MORE

▶ Think about your life. Is there anyone you need to forgive?

▶ Find Matthew 18:21–22. How many times does the Bible say you should forgive someone who offends you? Do you believe the Bible literally has a number in mind, or do you think there's a principle involved? If so, what is it?

▶ Why does it matter whether we forgive or not? Read Matthew 6:14–15.

75

¡ASPIRE TO KILL BITTERNESS

Put out of your life all these things: bad feelings about other people, anger, temper, loud talk, bad talk which hurts other people, and bad feelings which hurt other people.

EPHESIANS 4:31

When someone really hurts you and you refuse to forgive, bitterness develops. That is anger festering in your heart unchecked.

Imagine finding a container of food that got shoved under the seat of your car for a long time. The food is completely rotten. It stinks and it's covered in mold, and you can't even tell what kind of food it was originally. Disgusting, right?

That's what bitterness looks like in our hearts. When anger and hurt are hidden instead of handled, we get rotten inside. And many people have been completely destroyed by bitterness.

So it's a kind and gracious thing that God requires us to forgive those who hurt us.

Instead of being bitter, here's what the Bible tells us to do:

Be at peace with all men. Live a holy life. No one will see the Lord without having that kind of life. See that no one misses God's loving-favor. Do not let wrong thoughts about others get started among you. If you do, many people will be turned to a life of sin.

HEBREWS 12:14–15

God loves you too much to allow bitterness, even over legitimately hurtful things, to destroy your life. He purchased your life with the blood of His only beloved Son, and He has a plan for your life that is far greater than you could imagine for yourself. So He tells you to fight life-killing, soul-destroying bitterness with forgiveness.

When you choose forgiveness over bitterness, you're not pretending the hurt never happened. Laying down the bitterness simply means you choose obedience to God. In return, He will pick up the wrong you've experienced and handle it according to His will.

Your heavenly Father never tells you to disregard your hurt. He never even tells you to forget it (though He Himself forgets the sins He forgives). Instead, God just tells you to forgive and let Him handle the rest.

Aspire to kill bitterness.

¡ASPIRE TO KNOW MORE

- ▶ Find Romans 12:19. What will God do to someone who wrongs you?

- ▶ Read Matthew 18:23–35. Read this parable of a man who was forgiven a great debt but then was unwilling to extend the same mercy to someone in a smaller way. How does this parable address bitterness and forgiveness?

76

¡ASPIRE TO LOVE MY ENEMIES

*"But love those who hate you. Do good to them. Let them use
your things and do not expect something back. Your reward will
be much. You will be the children of the Most High. He is kind to
those who are not thankful and to those who are full of sin."*

LUKE 6:35

God tells us to do a lot of hard things. Loving our enemies may be one of the hardest.

People can do unimaginably bad things to each other. But God calls us to love our enemies, so we have to assume this is for our good and His glory.

What does it look like to love our enemies? Does it mean we don't care what they've done? Does it mean we have to ignore our hurt feelings? Does it mean we look the other way when people do wrong? No, not at all.

To help us understand this idea of loving our enemies, Jesus provided two great examples.

First, during His last supper with the disciples, knowing that Judas was about betray Him, what did Jesus do?

*Jesus got up from the supper and took off His
coat. He picked up a cloth and put it around Him.
Then He put water into a wash pan and began
to wash the feet of His followers.*

JOHN 13:4–5

The Lord willingly washed the feet of the one who would betray Him! Jesus didn't justify Judas. He didn't pretend that what Judas was doing was okay. But instead of lashing out or treating Judas the way he "deserved" to be treated, Jesus served him.

Second, on the cross, Jesus did the same thing for us.

It's easy to think that the Lord died for us because we're basically nice and we love Him. And, hey—wouldn't you die for someone like yourself? No, it just doesn't work that way. The Bible tells us that before we knew God, we were His *enemies*:

> *We hated God. But we were saved from*
> *the punishment of sin by the death of Christ.*
> Romans 5:10

Jesus' death on the cross wasn't just an act of love for "the world"; it was a demonstration of love for His *enemies*. And it was a display of love for His Father, who had planned salvation before He even created the world. When we love our enemies, we're actually loving God, because loving our enemies is ultimately obedience to Him.

God understands how it feels and what it costs to love enemies. He's not telling us to do anything that He hasn't already done. If we love others the way God loves us, we'll love no matter what they do. And we'll look a lot like Jesus as we do.

¡ASPIRE TO KNOW MORE

▶ Find 1 John 4:19. According to this verse, why do you love Jesus?

▶ Think about the people in your life. Is there anyone you would consider an enemy? What can you do today to love that person (or those people) like Christ loves them?

77

¡ASPIRE TO GIVE GRACE

He who loves a pure heart and is kind in
his speaking has the king as his friend.
PROVERBS 22:11

Since you woke up this morning, you have been given more grace by your heavenly Father than you've received from anybody else in your entire lifetime.

Grace can be defined as undeserved or unearned kindness.

Our God—the one, true God—is a grace-giving God.

Some researchers estimate there are more than four thousand religions in the world. In all but one of them, people must work to earn the love and favor of their god or gods. Some adherents do extreme things—such as hurt themselves or abandon people they love—to impress their false gods. And many of these worshippers are never given any guarantee that their deity will be pleased with the hard things they've done.

But your true and living God did something no false god has ever done or will ever do.

God showed His love to us. While we
were still sinners, Christ died for us.
ROMANS 5:8

Long before you knew about God or chose to follow Him, He already loved you. He sent His only Son to die for you. When there was nothing but sin in your heart, God wanted you to be His child. Just stop and think about that for a moment: even before you ever heard the name *Jesus*, He loved you—and He did more for you than anyone else ever will.

That is grace. Grace is doing something good for someone else who doesn't deserve it or hasn't done anything to earn it.

So what should you do with the incredible grace you've been given? Show grace to others.

Every day, you have many opportunities to show grace—undeserved, unearned kindness—to other people. They have bad days and make bad decisions. They do and say hurtful things. They care mainly about themselves and don't even think about you or your needs. But in each of these cases, we have an opportunity to show people the love of Christ by passing along the grace of God that we've been given.

> *Let your conversation be always full of grace, seasoned with salt, so that you may know how to answer everyone.*
> COLOSSIANS 4:6 NIV

Aspire to understand the grace you've been given by God. As you realize how much He's done, it becomes easier to give grace to other people.

¡ASPIRE TO KNOW MORE

▶ Read Romans 11:6. Do we receive grace from God because we deserve it?

▶ Find Ephesians 4:29-32, verses describing the type of person who shows grace to others. Is there any aspect from these verses that you need to work on this week?

▶ Keeping in mind that *grace* is doing good for a person who doesn't deserve it, who is someone you should show grace to today?

78

¡ASPIRE TO DO GOD'S WILL

May God give you every good thing you need so you can do what
He wants. May He do in us what pleases Him through Jesus Christ.
May Christ have all the shining-greatness forever! Let it be so.

HEBREWS 13:21

God's will for your life is easier to find than you may think.

Sometimes we make His will for our lives harder to understand than it needs to be. We want to know what the entire future holds—what we should study in college, what job we should pursue, what person we should marry—but God doesn't often (or even usually) give us all the details at once. Sometimes, even when we *think* we know those details, they change unexpectedly. So God usually gives us what we need to know when we need to know it. And He just wants us to trust Him with the rest.

In the meantime, His will for our lives is simple: obey Him. And here are three things He tells you to do:

Rejoice always, pray without ceasing,
give thanks in all circumstances; for this
is the will of God in Christ Jesus for you.

1 THESSALONIANS 5:16–18 ESV

Doing God's will is as simple—and as challenging—as rejoicing, praying, and giving thanks.

You may have your future figured out. You may know with confidence what you want to do and where you want to go. If so, great. But remember to trust God if there are twists and turns in your journey ahead. It's in those twists and turns that you'll have opportunities to find God is completely trustworthy. And pleasing Him is always more important than achieving any goal.

You may have no idea what your future holds. You may not know what you want to do next or where you should go. If so, that's okay too. Trust that God knows what's best for your life and that He will lead you to the right thing at the right time. Pray faithfully. Ask God for wisdom. Consider carefully the skills, talents, and interests He's given you and how you could use them to help others. God is even more interested in your future than you are, so trust Him with it.

If you love and obey God, you can't miss His will for your life. As you trust Him—listening to the counsel of those who love both God and you—each step of your life will become clear at the right time.

iASPIRE TO KNOW MORE

▶ Find Romans 12:2. According to this verse, what are some steps you can take to learn what God wants you to do with your life?

▶ Read Proverbs 15:22. Who do you know that loves both God and you? Talk to this person this week about God's will for your life.

79

¡ASPIRE TO WORK HARD

*Whatever work you do, do it with all your
heart. Do it for the Lord and not for men.*

COLOSSIANS 3:23

No matter what job you do, no matter who your boss is, you're really working for God. First Corinthians 10:31 says, "So if you eat or drink or whatever you do, do everything to honor God."

Sometimes in life we have to do jobs we don't enjoy. Maybe they're chores around the house or homework for a school subject we don't like. Sometimes we'll work for bosses, teachers, or even parents who are unkind. But none of this should change how hard we work or how committed we are to doing a good job, because, ultimately, we answer to God.

A boss, teacher, or parent may be unfairly critical or too easily impressed. But God can see your heart, and He knows whether or not you're doing your best job.

If we aren't working as hard as we should, if we're not living up to our full potential, answering to God can be bad news. But if we are truly doing our best, He is pleased, no matter what any other person might think.

How exactly do we work hard? Do we have to put in a certain amount of time? Are we trying to earn a boss's full approval? Does it require straight As in school? Not necessarily.

Working hard for the Lord means we ask ourselves questions such as "How would God want me to complete this work?" "How would Jesus do this job if He were here?" "How can I glorify God with what I am doing?"

One great thing about working for the Lord is that He will help us complete each task. It's always good to begin a new duty by praying for God's help. He is more than able to give us the strength, wisdom, and ability to do the tasks required of us.

Trust your work to the Lord,
and your plans will work out well.
PROVERBS 16:3

Whatever the outcome of your job—whether your boss, teacher, or parent is happy or not—God will reward you if you've done your best.

Remember that you will get your reward from
the Lord. He will give you what you should
receive. You are working for the Lord Christ.
COLOSSIANS 3:24

Aspire to work hard—for the Lord.

¡ASPIRE TO KNOW MORE

▶ Proverbs 6:6–8 tells us to watch and learn from whom? (Hint: She probably doesn't come to mind when you think of hard workers.)

▶ Find Ecclesiastes 9:10. How much effort should you put into your work?

▶ Read Philippians 2:14–15. According to these verses, how should we do our work?

iASPIRE TO TAKE RESPONSIBILITY

If you are wise, your wisdom is a help to you.
If you laugh at the truth, you alone will suffer for it.
PROVERBS 9:12

Responsibility is a big word that simply means doing your duty with a good attitude.

The older we get, the more responsibilities we have. When you were a baby, for example, you didn't have any responsibility. As a toddler, your biggest duty was probably sharing your toys. Now that you're growing up, you're probably responsible for homework, good behavior, and keeping your room clean. In several years, you'll have even more responsibilities. Lord willing, you may be responsible for a career or a family.

Wanting more responsibility is a good thing—it shows your desire to grow and mature. We shouldn't want to be children for the rest of our lives. Accepting responsibility is one way we please God.

As a young boy growing into a man, even Jesus had to take on responsibility. The New Testament writer Luke described His growth this way:

Jesus grew strong in mind and body.
He grew in favor with God and men.
LUKE 2:52

Becoming responsible like Jesus did begins with taking responsibility for *yourself*. Here are three simple ways you can do that:

First, *take control of your thoughts, words, and actions*. Those things don't just happen to us. We *choose* what we're going to think, say, and do. Making wise choices is one way we take responsibility.

Second, *stop blaming other people for your decisions*. "It's not my fault!" shouldn't be our first reaction when something goes wrong. When we blame other people for choices we've made, we're making ourselves victims of our circumstances. That means we think everything is done *to us* without our permission. But blaming other people does nothing to make us better, stronger, or more like Jesus.

Third, *refuse to complain.* Complaining is just a creative way to deflect responsibility when something doesn't go as planned. When bad things happen, we grow if we consider what we can do better next time. When we choose to learn instead of complain, even our mistakes become gifts.

As a young man on earth, Jesus took responsibility, and He pleased His Father. Aspire to accept responsibility, and you'll please God too.

¡ASPIRE TO KNOW MORE

▶ Find Romans 15:1. What does this verse say about our responsibility to other people?

▶ Read Ecclesiastes 12:13–14. According to these verses, what is our main responsibility?

▶ Of the three ways for taking responsibility listed above, which one can you work on this week? Ask God to help you do it.

81

¡ASPIRE TO FACE FAILURE

He answered me, "I am all you need. I give you My loving-favor.
My power works best in weak people." I am happy to be weak
and have troubles so I can have Christ's power in me.

2 CORINTHIANS 12:9

Ever feel discouraged about mistakes you've made?

Did you know that, since you're a child of God, your mistakes and failures can still be used in God's big plan for your life? Because He knows everything, He knew everything that would happen in your life, and His plans for your future are still right on schedule.

Failure doesn't need to be fatal.

One of Jesus' closest friends was the disciple Peter. You get the impression he was loud and outgoing, probably the kind of guy who never met a stranger. Everything Peter did was big, and he loved Jesus. So imagine Peter's surprise when Jesus told him, "For sure, I tell you, before a rooster crows this night, you will say three times you do not know Me" (Matthew 26:34).

No way! Peter thought. And then he made a boastful promise to his Lord:

> *"Even if I have to die with You,*
> *I will never say I do not know You."*
> MATTHEW 26:35

No doubt Peter meant every word. He loved Jesus; why would he deny knowing Him?

But then the most horrible night in history unfolded. Judas sold out Jesus, who was soon arrested. Events began escalating quickly. Outside the home of the Jewish high priest, someone accused Peter of being a follower of Jesus.

Have you ever been singled out for something, and in a moment of panic, you lied?

Three times Peter denied following Jesus. The third time he even cursed his accusers. And then the rooster crowed. When he realized what he had done, Peter broke down and wept.

That could have been the end of Peter's story. No doubt, Peter's choices hurt Jesus. But God is faithful, and He used Peter in spite of his failures. Peter was the first disciple Jesus appeared to after His resurrection. Peter became a leader of the early church, which God used him to jump-start. It was Peter's sermon in Acts 2 that caused three thousand people to trust Christ for salvation. God wasn't done with Peter because of his failure—even one so big.

Sometimes, we do things so dumb and embarrassing we think we'll never be able to recover. But they could actually be great gifts in our lives. God is remarkable at taking our weaknesses, struggles, and failings and using them in powerful ways for good.

Failing isn't the worst thing you can do. Refusing to confess your sin, submit to God, and let Him use your failure for good. . .now *that's* the worst thing you can do.

¡ASPIRE TO KNOW MORE

▶ Read John 21:1–14. In this chapter, Jesus talks to His disciples after the resurrection. What does Peter's response to Jesus tell you about his response to his recent failure?

▶ If you've failed in some way and struggle to move forward, pray and give the error to God, trusting that He will use it in your life for good.

82

¡ASPIRE TO REDEFINE SUCCESS

Trust your work to the Lord,
and your plans will work out well.
PROVERBS 16:3

People love success. Even more, people love *talking* about success.

You can take classes, attend seminars, and read books by countless "experts" who will tell you what it means to be successful in life. And every one of them will offer a different strategy for how to achieve success.

Spoiler alert: many (if not most) will tell you that true success looks like happiness, money, appreciation, comfort, or confidence.

Being happy, having money, being appreciated, enjoying comfort, and feeling confident are not sinful things. God gives good gifts, and He can decide how and when to bless His children in different ways.

But if you make things like happiness, money, and comfort your biggest goals, you'll likely reach the end of your life and know with certainty that you missed out on something much better. Many "successful" people have.

In the Old Testament, after Moses died, Joshua took leadership of the Israelites. God told him,

> *"This Book of the Law shall not depart from your*
> *mouth, but you shall meditate on it day and night,*
> *so that you may be careful to do according to all*
> *that is written in it. For then you will make your way*
> *prosperous, and then you will have good success."*
> JOSHUA 1:8 ESV

God measured Joshua's success—as He measures ours—according to *obedience*, not any particular result. He's in charge of results. We're just expected to trust and obey.

When we care more about results than obeying God, we easily try to manipulate things. We care more about how successful we look to others than about what God is doing in our hearts. But He isn't fooled by what we pretend to be, even if we're convincing to other people.

God defines success as obeying His Word. It's as simple—and as challenging—as obedience. Aspire to redefine success.

¡ASPIRE TO KNOW MORE

▶ Read Psalm 1:1-3 to see what success looks like for a Christian.

▶ Look up Proverbs 3:1-4. Note the list of what God requires in order for you to be successful. Do any of the items on this list depend on talent, intelligence, or popularity?

83

¡ASPIRE TO BE CONTENT

A God-like life gives us much when
we are happy for what we have.

1 TIMOTHY 6:6

Things will never satisfy your heart. Not a new car, not a better job, not more money. Not even a girlfriend or boyfriend or husband or wife! These things and many others can be gifts from God, who truly loves to give good things to His children. But none of them will ever solve your greatest problems or meet your deepest needs.

Strangely enough, as wonderful as they may be, new cars, better jobs, more money, and loving relationships all come with additional problems and challenges. It is only the Creator—not anything He's made—that will fill the void in your heart.

Jesus died on the cross to rescue you from the punishment for sin, but also from thinking you can seek physically what can only be found spiritually. If you learn this truth while you're still young, you'll save yourself lots of grief as you get older.

Your greatest need right now is the same as your greatest need the day you called out to God to save you. Your greatest need every day is Jesus Christ.

And now that you have Him, you have no reason to be discontent.

But discontentment is nothing new. Two millennia ago, as crowds of people gathered to hear Jesus speak, this is what He said:

> *"Watch yourselves! Keep from wanting all kinds*
> *of things you should not have. A man's life is not*
> *made up of things, even if he has many riches."*

LUKE 12:15

The warning still applies to us today.

If we're not content with what we have right now, what makes us think we'll be happy when we get more? After we get the next thing, we'll probably just want something else.

It's easy to desire newer, bigger, or better things. And it's easy to measure our worth—or the worth of people in our lives—based on possessions. Isn't our tendency to respect people with lots of money? And when we daydream about the future, we don't typically think about having *less* stuff, do we? Generally, we want more.

Sometimes contentment is less about what we own and more about *what owns us*; that is, maybe you don't spend your time wishing you had something else, but is there anything in your life that you just couldn't live without?

Here's the secret to being content: instead of looking at what your friends have, look at all God has already given you. When you keep your eyes on Him, you'll realize you have more than enough.

¡ASPIRE TO KNOW MORE

▶ First Timothy 6:8 lists only two things we need in order to be content. What are they?

▶ Is something you don't have keeping you from being content with the life God has given you? If so, what is it? Pray and ask God to fill that longing with Himself.

▶ Can you think of three things you've never thanked God for that you *can* thank Him for today?

iASPIRE TO REST WEEKLY

Jesus said to them, "The Day of Rest was made for the good of man. Man was not made for the Day of Rest."

MARK 2:27

Have you ever considered why your game controllers, music players, and video devices have both PAUSE and STOP buttons? *Pause* generally means you're taking a short break with every intention of coming back soon. *Stop* means you're ending something for an undetermined amount of time—maybe even forever.

Did you know that God wants you to take a pause every week?

Back in Genesis 1, we read that God created the world. In a spectacular display of power, He created everything out of nothing simply by speaking things into existence. But then, after six days of creating the universe and everything in it, He did something that seems unusual for an all-powerful God: He rested.

On the seventh day God ended His work which He had done. And He rested on the seventh day from all His work which He had done. Then God honored the seventh day and made it holy, because in it He rested from all His work which He had done.

GENESIS 2:2–3

What did God do on the seventh day? He took a pause. This pause had nothing to do with how much energy or ability God had. If anyone could afford *not* to rest, it was Him. God never, ever gets tired or runs out of power.

But He rested, at least in part, to demonstrate what He wants *us* to do. The day of rest was made for the good of people.

In Exodus 20, God gave Moses ten major commandments to pass on to the children of Israel. These commandments are still important today because they give us insight into God's heart and what He wants from His children. Every commandment is included for a reason.

The third one says,

> "Remember the Day of Rest, to keep it holy. Six
> days you will do all your work. But the seventh
> day is a Day of Rest to the Lord your God."
>
> EXODUS 20:8–10

We don't live under Old Testament laws today, so we have great freedom to decide when and how to rest. But the truth remains: it's a good idea to rest weekly.

Because it's traditionally the day of worship, Sunday is a good day to set aside. Make the day different than any other day of the week.

Not only is this a gift to you, but it brings glory to God. Aspire to pause. Aspire to rest like God Himself did.

¡ASPIRE TO KNOW MORE

▶ Find Matthew 11:28. When you are tired and in need of rest, where should you go?

▶ What could you start doing to honor God on a rest day? Here are some ideas: spend extra time reading your Bible or praying, listen to music about God, be still and think about God's goodness.

85

¡ASPIRE TO GIVE CHEERFULLY

*He is filled with desire all day long, but the
man who is right with God gives all he can.*
PROVERBS 21:26

God loves cheerful givers. Throughout the Bible, God demonstrates a pattern of giving generously to His people and then blessing them when they give generously in return. But He doesn't bless givers who give in order to be blessed—God blesses givers who give *to please Him.*

God isn't a vending machine. We don't put money into the church's offering plate hoping to get money back from God. We don't give to the poor expecting God to give us twice as much as we gave away. Despite what some preachers on television like to say, God doesn't work like that. Giving in order to get isn't generous—it's selfish.

We should give because it's just another way to honor the God who generously gives to us.

*Each man should give as he has decided in his heart.
He should not give, wishing he could keep it. Or he
should not give if he feels he has to give. God loves a man
who gives because he wants to give. God can give you
all you need. He will give you more than enough. You
will have everything you need for yourselves. And you
will have enough left over when there is a need.*
2 CORINTHIANS 9:7–8

You may not have much money to give right now. You might not even have a job yet or any money coming in on a regular basis. If so, here are some things to do until you're making money:

First, purpose in your heart that when God does bless you with money in the future, you will be faithful to give back to Him. Oftentimes, giving to God sounds like a great idea—until you start thinking of all the other fun things you could do with the money. But there is truly no better way to handle your money than giving some of it back to God. Whatever you keep for yourself will be temporary, but whatever you give to God will last for eternity.

Second, start being generous in other ways. Money isn't the only thing you can give generously. The emphasis in the Bible is on giving what you have, and that can be time, energy, or talent. You can invest in the lives of other people by being a friend or by serving in ministry. Your generosity will please God.

> *Do not neglect to do good and to share what*
> *you have, for such sacrifices are pleasing to God.*
> HEBREWS 13:16 ESV

It has rightly been said by many, "You can give without loving, but you cannot love without giving."

So aspire to give—generously and cheerfully.

iASPIRE TO KNOW MORE

- ▶ Find Acts 20:35. According to Jesus, what is better than receiving things?

- ▶ Are you a cheerful giver? If not, what can you start giving generously to God?

86

¡ASPIRE TO DO WHAT MATTERS

One thing I have asked from the Lord, that I will look for: that I
may live in the house of the Lord all the days of my life, to look
upon the beauty of the Lord, and to worship in His holy house.

PSALM 27:4

Many things matter in life. It matters whether you do your best in school, whether you're a good friend and family member, whether you live up to your full potential on the job, and whether you're faithful to your church.

Life is full of things that matter, but one thing matters *most*:

"You must love the Lord your God with all
your heart and with all your soul and with
all your mind and with all your strength."

MARK 12:30

Nothing in life is as important as your relationship with God.

Throughout the Bible, we read stories of people who did important things. There's David killing Goliath, Esther saving her people, John baptizing Jesus, and Peter walking on water. And after reading these stories, we may want to do big, amazing things for Jesus too. It's good to want to make a difference for the cause of Christ. If God calls you to do something exciting with your life, do it for His glory!

But if we read the Bible stories carefully, we also learn that one thing matters most: to love and seek after God with our whole heart. All the rest is just detail in our story.

Today, in countries like Pakistan, people who follow Jesus are treated as outcasts. As a result, many Christians are only able to find work as servants, street sweepers, and sewage workers. Can you imagine spending your entire adult life climbing in and out of a dirty sewer all day just because you choose to worship Jesus? No doubt many Christians in Pakistan are brilliant, talented people who, if it weren't for their faith, could pursue any career they wanted.

Most of us aspire to respected, well-paying jobs. But in Pakistan, for those who've chosen to follow Jesus, working in sewers or sweeping streets is doing what matters. In fact, many Pakistani Christians accept these jobs with joy because it means they have chosen the one needful thing—to follow their Lord.

Everything in life becomes important when serving the One who is most important. The apostle Paul said it this way:

> I hope very much that I will have no reason to
> be ashamed. I hope to honor Christ with my
> body if it be by my life or by my death. I want
> to honor Him without fear, now and always.
>
> PHILIPPIANS 1:20

Aspire to do what matters—to honor God in every area of your life.

¡ASPIRE TO KNOW MORE

▶ With your parents' permission, go to www.persecution.com/globalprayerguide/pakistan to learn how to pray for your Christian brothers and sisters in Pakistan.

▶ Do you remember the story of the sisters Mary and Martha in Luke 10? How did Jesus gently correct the overworked Martha in verses 41 and 42?

87

¡ASPIRE TO LIVE BOLDLY

What, then, shall we say in response to these things?
If God is for us, who can be against us?
ROMANS 8:31 NIV

You have only one life. Live it boldly.

But, you may ask, what does living boldly look like?

Living with Christian boldness means taking good risks for God: praying boldly, trusting boldly, giving the Gospel boldly, and loving boldly.

We do not glorify God with timidity, being afraid of stepping out in faith or failing to share the good news of the Gospel with people in need. We do not please God by asking Him to meet our needs and then doubting that He will provide.

When we remember what God has already done for us and what He promises to do in the future, we can live boldly for Him.

We can come to God without fear
because we have put our trust in Christ.
EPHESIANS 3:12

If you look throughout history, you'll find that the men and women God used most mightily are the ones who believed His promises. They found courage to do bold things by believing what they read in their Bibles, verses like,

I know that nothing can keep us from the love of God. Death
cannot! Life cannot! Angels cannot! Leaders cannot! Any other
power cannot! Hard things now or in the future cannot! The
world above or the world below cannot! Any other living thing

cannot keep us away from the love of God
which is ours through Christ Jesus our Lord.
ROMANS 8:38-39

The book of Acts tells the story of the early church. By chapter 4, Jesus had already returned to heaven to live with His Father. The disciples in and around Jerusalem knew that sharing the Gospel could get them persecuted. . .or killed. Nobody—including Jesus' disciples—wants to experience pain and death.

So did the disciples hide? Did they run away? No, they prayed for boldness. And here is exactly what they said:

"Make it easy for your servants to preach Your Word with power. May you heal and do powerful works and special things to see through the name of Jesus, Your Holy Son!"
ACTS 4:29-30

The disciples asked God for courage to live boldly, and God answered their prayer. He wanted them to live boldly, and He wants you to live the same way.

You have one life. Aspire to live boldly for the glory of God.

¡ASPIRE TO KNOW MORE

▶ When we truly believe the promises of God, our fears begin to disappear. We may still feel nervous from time to time, but we have the Bible to answer our doubts. What is a promise of God you can trust today?

▶ Find Ephesians 6:18-20. What did the apostle Paul ask the Ephesian Christians to pray for on his behalf?

88

¡ASPIRE TO MAKE A DIFFERENCE

When you are around people who do not know God,
be careful how you act. Even if they talk against you as
wrong-doers, in the end they will give thanks to God
for your good works when Christ comes again.

1 PETER 2:12

Making a difference with your life is easier than you may think. You don't have to be the smartest, the funniest, or the most talented. You don't need to be famous or even well-liked! You simply have to be obedient to what God tells you to do. If you pour out your life for God and the Gospel, *you will make a difference.*

You may not see or understand the full impact of your life until eternity. But be assured of this: if you serve God faithfully wherever He puts you, you will make a difference.

Here's how Jesus describes it:

> *"Let your light shine in front of men. Then they*
> *will see the good things you do and will*
> *honor your Father Who is in heaven."*

MATTHEW 5:16

Part of living for God and the Gospel is simply being the same person no matter where you are or what you're doing. Human beings are very good at figuring out when another person is being phony. And being phony is one of the best ways to *not* make a difference.

Why would we have different versions of ourselves? Sadly, there are times when we tolerate different levels of sin based on who we're with.

For example, if you use language with schoolmates that you would never use with people at church, you're tolerating the sin of corrupt communication in one place but not another. If you're willing to lose your temper at home but you know better than to blow up at school, you're tolerating the sins of selfishness and anger in one place but not another.

We should be the same person everywhere we go, and we should refuse to tolerate sin in any context.

If you ever notice that you're changing your behavior based on where you are or who you're with, ask God to show you why. Specifically, pray with the psalm writer,

> *Look through me, O God, and know my heart. Try me*
> *and know my thoughts. See if there is any sinful way*
> *in me and lead me in the way that lasts forever.*
> PSALM 139:23–24

God wants you to make a difference with your life, and He's willing and able to help you accomplish that goal. Aspire to glorify Him by your life of integrity.

¡ASPIRE TO KNOW MORE

▶ Find Philippians 3:7–11 to see how the apostle Paul made a difference with his life for the glory of God.

▶ Before you can make a difference with your life, you must decide what your goal in life is. Do you want to please yourself or do you want to please God? Read Philippians 3:14 to see Paul's goal for his life.

89

¡ASPIRE TO LOVE WITHOUT REGRET

*Dear friends, let us love each other, because love
comes from God. Those who love are God's
children and they know God.*

1 JOHN 4:7

Loving without regret isn't the same thing as loving without getting hurt. In fact, when we love people the way Jesus does, we'll sometimes get taken advantage of—and that doesn't feel good. But loving people the way Christ loves them means we love wholeheartedly, caring more about their relationship with God than their opinion of us.

One of the people Jesus poured His earthly life and ministry into was Judas Iscariot. He was one of the original twelve disciples with whom Jesus spent a *lot* of time. Jesus ate with them, prayed with them, ministered with them, and lived with them. What an incredible privilege for the disciples!

Can you imagine getting to talk to Jesus face-to-face anytime you wanted? Crowds of people desperately sought the Lord's attention for a few minutes, but the disciples had it for three years. And yet one of them—Judas Iscariot—ended up betraying Jesus for thirty pieces of silver.

In other parts of the New Testament (such as Matthew 20), we see that a piece of silver was considered a day's pay. So thirty pieces of silver was roughly six weeks' worth of income. So even after Jesus poured His life into Judas, Judas was willing to sell Him out for today's equivalent of about five thousand dollars.

That might sound like a lot of money to a teenager. But if you're an adult paying bills, you know it doesn't go nearly as far as you want it to. And it's certainly a tiny sum compared to the value of a friendship with Jesus. When given the choice, Judas loved money more than he loved his Lord.

But here's perhaps the most shocking part of this story: since Jesus is omniscient—a big word that means He knows everything—He already knew that Judas would betray Him. In fact, Jesus knew that long before He even invited Judas to be part of the twelve disciples. Yet Jesus welcomed Him anyway.

Jesus loved and served His betrayer *even on the day of the betrayal.*

If Jesus could love the people who put Him on the cross, we ought to love those who hurt us far less. You will never regret loving people the way Christ loves them, even if you're taken advantage of. . .even if your kindness isn't returned. . .even if the friendship eventually falls apart.

Here is Jesus' own command:

> *"I give you a new Law. You are to love each other.*
> *You must love each other as I have loved you. If you love each*
> *other, all men will know you are My followers."*
>
> JOHN 13:34–35

To know what it looks like to love without regret, look to Jesus.

¡ASPIRE TO KNOW MORE

▶ Find John 6:67–71. According to these verses, did Judas decide to be a disciple of Jesus, or did Jesus choose him?

▶ Who is someone in your life that you can choose to love like Jesus does?

90

¡ASPIRE TO RETHINK BEAUTY

Your beauty should come from the inside. It should come
from the heart. This is the kind that lasts. Your beauty
should be a gentle and quiet spirit. In God's sight this is
of great worth and no amount of money can buy it.

1 PETER 3:4

Did you know beauty is both subjective and objective?

Beauty is *subjective*, which means we get to have different opinions, tastes, and feelings about what we think looks nice. Take a piece of bold art, for example, and you'll probably find people who love it and hate it. That's okay—God made us with unique perspectives. We don't all need to agree on what makes beautiful art.

Beauty is also *objective*, which means there are right and wrong answers about it. As Creator of the universe, God is the author of beauty. So when He inspired the apostle Peter to define beauty in the New Testament, we should pay attention:

Do not let your beauty come from the outside.
It should not be the way you comb your hair or the
wearing of gold or the wearing of fine clothes. Your
beauty should come from the inside. It should come
from the heart. This is the kind that lasts. Your beauty
should be a gentle and quiet spirit. In God's sight this
is of great worth and no amount of money can buy it.

1 PETER 3:3-4

When it comes to things like art, we get to decide what we like. But when we think of beauty in people, God has given us His standard—and

He says the *heart* matters most.

Does this mean we shouldn't fix our hair or wear nice clothes? Of course not. But we should care more about what's happening in our own hearts than anything else.

Rethinking beauty is important both for what we see in the world and what we see in the mirror. Far more important than your clothes, your haircut, or your jewelry is your heart. Who are you, really?

Anybody can pay money to look nice, but nobody can pay money to have a good heart. That is God's desire for us, and we can pray the biblical words David wrote:

> *Make a clean heart in me, O God.*
> *Give me a new spirit that will not be moved.*
> PSALM 51:10

Really, we should be far more concerned with how God sees us than with the way any other person does. That's why we can't look to other people—in the media, online, or among our friends—to define beauty. So many people base their understanding of "beauty" on everything but what God says. To be beautiful yourself and to be attracted to what is beautiful, look to God and His Word.

Everything that is truly beautiful points to God.

¡ASPIRE TO KNOW MORE

▶ According to Proverbs 31:30, what ultimately becomes of outward beauty?

▶ Read Proverbs 4:20–23 to see what God's Word says about your inner thoughts and feelings.

91

¡ASPIRE TO GUARD MY HEART

*Keep your heart pure for out of it
are the important things of life.*
PROVERBS 4:23

Have you ever locked away something that was important to you? Maybe you stashed money or jewelry in a safe deposit box at the bank so nobody could steal it. Or perhaps you write in a diary or journal that has a built-in lock so no one can read your private thoughts.

We lock away things we want to protect.

How about your heart?

The verse above, Proverbs 4:23, can also be translated this way:

*Above all else, guard your heart,
for everything you do flows from it (NIV).*

When God tells you to "guard your heart," He's saying, "lock it up and keep it safe."

Of course, we're not talking about the blood-pumping organ in your chest—we're referring to the mission control center of our emotions, affections, and feelings. Our heart is the core of who we are and what we think. And it is vastly important.

Jesus explained it this way:

*"Good comes from a good man because of
the riches he has in his heart. Sin comes from a
sinful man because of the sin he has in his heart.
The mouth speaks of what the heart is full of."*

LUKE 6:45

If your heart is full of love for God, then your words, actions, and attitudes will glorify Him. But if your heart is full of pride and sin, then your words, actions, and attitudes will cause great harm to yourself and others.

God wants you to guard your heart. Here are three ways to do that:

First, *pay attention to what's in your heart*. Pay attention to what you're thinking, feeling, and saying. If you notice sinful patterns in your life, trace your actions back to particular thoughts, feelings, and desires.

Second, *weigh everything in your heart against what the Bible says*. As followers of Jesus, we must submit our desires to God and His Word. When we recognize that we want things the Bible tells us not to want, we must willingly set those desires aside for the glory of God.

Finally, *talk to God about what's in your heart*. Nobody cares more about protecting your heart than God does, so ask Him to show you what's in your heart and what needs to be corrected.

Your heart is the most important thing about you. Aspire to guard it well.

¡ASPIRE TO KNOW MORE

▶ Read 1 Thessalonians 2:4. This verse is part of a letter Paul wrote as he was traveling from city to city to share the Gospel. According to this verse, who tests and proves our heart?

▶ Read Jeremiah 17:9. The world will tell you to *follow your heart*. According to this verse, why is that a bad idea?

92

¡ASPIRE TO FIGHT ADDICTION

I am allowed to do all things, but not everything is good for me
to do! Even if I am free to do all things, I will not do them if I
think it would be hard for me to stop when I know I should.

1 CORINTHIANS 6:12

When you hear the word *addiction*, what comes to mind?

Maybe you think about cigarettes, vaping, alcohol, or drugs. And you wouldn't be wrong. Many people in our world are addicted to harmful substances. If you or someone you love ever find yourself trapped by substance abuse, aspire to fight that addiction. First, ask God for help—He's willing and able to give you everything you need, and even better, He's ready to fight with and for you. Second, talk to a parent or another trusted adult who can help with your battle. Don't ever let pride stand in the way of getting help.

The apostle Paul, in 1 Corinthians 7:23, tells us that Jesus bought us with a great price, so we should not be dependent on anything or anyone but Him. Unfortunately, because we're human, all of us struggle with some form of addiction.

An addiction is just something we go to for release or relief when we're sad, mad, or otherwise unhappy. Addictions are anything that controls us. Here are some examples that might surprise you: food, friends, gaming, movies, music, sleep.

These things aren't all bad. In fact, they can be great gifts from God. But food, friends, gaming, movies, music, and sleep should never *replace* God.

So where does He want us to turn when we are struggling?

Give all your cares to the Lord and He will
give you strength. He will never let those
who are right with Him be shaken.

PSALM 55:22

If you want to know what your particular addiction might be, watch where you turn when you're hurting or confused. If you go anywhere before you go to God, you may be addicted to that person or thing. And depending on anything other than God is sin.

So do not let sin have power over your body
here on earth. You must not obey the body
and let it do what it wants to do.

ROMANS 6:12

When something hard, sad, or frustrating happens in your life, go to God first. A new game, a long nap, or a funny movie may temporarily distract you from what you feel, but it won't ultimately help you. Only God can meet your deepest needs.

¡ASPIRE TO KNOW MORE

▶ According to 1 Peter 5:7, why should we go to God with things that upset or worry us?

▶ One way to learn whether or not something has become an addiction is to see what happens if you try to stop doing it for a while. If you find you can't let go of gaming or shopping or movies, for example, talk to God about what you should do next.

93

¡ASPIRE TO BE A GOOD STEWARD

A servant must be faithful to his owner.
This is expected of him.

1 CORINTHIANS 4:2

How often do you use the word *stewardship*? If someone asked, could you define it?

Whether you can put the idea into words, you probably put it into practice. And if you don't currently put it into practice, you absolutely have the ability to start doing so today!

When you handle your money carefully, or you take good care of your pet, or you recycle paper and plastic instead of just sticking it in the trash, you are being a steward—you're carefully and responsibly managing something that's been entrusted to you.

That's what the Bible means when it uses the word *stewardship*.

In 1 Corinthians 4, the apostle Paul described his responsibility to be a good steward of "the secrets of God" (v. 1). He did everything he could to share the good news of Jesus Christ that God had shared with him. In Paul's opinion, there was no place for laziness or carelessness when it came to preaching the Gospel. He took his responsibility seriously.

Throughout the Bible, we learn that stewardship applies to every area of our lives—from the way we spend our time to the way we handle our money to the way we treat the earth that God created.

Important note: We talk about stewarding things that belong to us, but in reality, everything we have has been given to us by God. They have been *entrusted* to us. So we are expected to take care of them responsibly.

God wants us to take what He's given and grow it—specifically, to develop or expand it in a way that benefits other people. Have you heard the story of the talents in Matthew 25? A talent was a measure of money used in biblical times. Sometimes a talent is referred to as "a bag of gold." In the New Testament, Jesus said that the kingdom of heaven is "like a man going on a journey, who called his servants and entrusted his wealth to them. To one he gave five bags of gold, to another two bags, and to another one bag, each according to his ability. Then he went on his journey. The man who had received five bags of gold went at once and put his money to work and gained five bags more. So also, the one with two bags of gold gained two more" (Matthew 25:14-17 NIV).

These men were commended and rewarded for their good stewardship. A third man, however, simply buried his bag of gold in the ground and was sharply criticized and punished (v. 24-30).

God has given you unique opportunities and skills, and He wants you to steward them wisely for the benefit of other people and ultimately for His glory. If you're unsure what God wants you to do, ask Him. He will gladly help you to "be faithful."

¡ASPIRE TO KNOW MORE

- ▶ Find 1 Corinthians 4:2 in other translations of the Bible or online at BibleGateway.com. How is stewardship presented? How does it help your understanding of *stewardship*?

- ▶ Read Luke 19:11-27, a similar story to the one in Matthew 25. If the overall story presents Jesus as king, what does verse 13 say about the things we have?

- ▶ Look up Matthew 12:36. How does this verse relate to the idea of stewardship?

¡ASPIRE TO EMBRACE CHANGE

*Jesus Christ is the same yesterday
and today and forever.*
HEBREWS 13:8

Change can be scary.

Human beings generally appreciate consistency and predictability. We like knowing what tomorrow will bring. Most of us feel safest when we have plans and when those plans are followed. But here's an unfortunate reality: very rarely does life go the way we planned.

Plans can change. People can change. Life can change. And it can happen in the blink of an eye.

It's been said that change is the only constant in life. Or, put another way, the only thing that doesn't change is change.

In the Bible, Joshua experienced a lot of change. Called by God to be Moses' assistant, Joshua was expected to fight battle after battle against powerful, scary armies. Because of a poor choice Moses made, God ultimately tapped Joshua to lead the Israelites into Canaan. It was a big responsibility to shepherd all those people into the land God had promised to them.

In the midst of all this change, Joshua was often and understandably fearful.

Seven times between Deuteronomy 31 and Joshua 1, Joshua is commanded to be strong and have courage. Whenever he was tempted to doubt that he could do what God was calling him to, Joshua got a heavenly reminder to be strong. In fact, the same words God spoke to Joshua could be applied to whatever the Lord calls *you* to do:

*"Have I not told you? Be strong and have strength
of heart! Do not be afraid or lose faith. For the
Lord your God is with you anywhere you go."*
JOSHUA 1:9

Many kids have been told they're moving to a new city. Others learn that they have to switch schools or churches. Any of us can go to bed one night and wake up the next day to what feels like a completely new life because of disappointing or devastating changes.

It's frustrating to feel like the ground beneath your feet is no longer solid. But here's good news: *Jesus never changes.*

He is the reason you can embrace whatever change enters your life.

The God who spoke the world into existence, parted the Red Sea for the Israelites, empowered David to defeat Goliath, talked with Moses on Mount Sinai, and raised the dead to life is the same God who will be your unmovable foundation in a world that always changes. He will be as faithful to you as He was to Joshua.

It is possible to embrace life's changes. Just hold tightly to the promises and character of our unchanging God.

¡ASPIRE TO KNOW MORE

▶ The last book of the Old Testament, Malachi, has only four chapters, but it contains seven of the most powerful words in the Bible. Find Malachi 3:6 to see what they are.

▶ Look up Proverbs 3:5-6. How might these verses relate to the changes of life?

▶ Read Psalm 46:1-3. Have you ever experienced the upheaval verses 2-3 describe? What is the answer in verse 1?

95

¡ASPIRE TO HOLD ON TO HOPE

*Hope never makes us ashamed because the love of God has come
into our hearts through the Holy Spirit Who was given to us.*

ROMANS 5:5

It is a powerful lie of the enemy that tries to convince us we are without hope.

No matter how hard or dark life can get, there is always, *always* hope for the person who holds fast to God. God is bigger than the worst circumstance we can imagine, and He is always able to turn things around. Broken relationships can be restored. Broken hearts can be mended. Broken bodies can be healed.

Our God is a big God who does big things. We honor Him by believing He can do what is impossible for us.

In Jesus' day, a Jewish religious leader named Jairus went to the Lord with an urgent matter:

> *He cried out to Jesus and said, "My little daughter
> is almost dead. Come and put Your hand on
> her that she may be healed and live."*

MARK 5:23

Can you imagine how anxious this dad must have been?

The Bible says Jesus started to go with Jairus. But there was a crowd following the Lord, and it seemed everyone wanted something from Him. In fact, Jesus had stopped to heal a woman in the crowd when a messenger came from Jairus's house announcing terrible news: the little girl had died.

Maybe you've lost someone you love, and you understand how devastating news like that is.

But what did Jesus say to Jairus in this horrible, hopeless moment? He said the same thing He says to any of us who are losing hope:

> *"Do not be afraid, just believe."*
>
> MARK 5:36

Maybe we say to ourselves, "But that doesn't make sense! I don't know how this could ever work out for good. I'm scared."

Never forget that God has pledged Himself to our good and His glory. That means—in every circumstance—He is aware of our situation and, even better, He is working the details together to accomplish His will. And that promise should always give us hope. The prophet Jeremiah, who knew all about hard situations, wrote,

> *But this I remember, and so I have hope. It is*
> *because of the Lord's loving-kindness that we*
> *are not destroyed for His loving-pity never ends.*
> *It is new every morning. He is so very faithful.*
>
> LAMENTATIONS 3:21–23

If you ever feel hopeless, remind yourself that God never wants you to think that way. The one who wants you to live without hope is the one who is hellbent on your destruction. Believing things are hopeless actually gives Satan the chance to do his worst work.

Aspire to hold on to hope.

¡ASPIRE TO KNOW MORE

▶ Read Mark 5:21–43 to see what happened to Jairus and his daughter.

▶ Find Romans 15:4. What, specifically, gives us strength and hope?

96

¡ASPIRE TO STAND FIRM

Be strong. Do not allow anyone to change your mind.
Always do your work well for the Lord. You know that
whatever you do for Him will not be wasted.

1 CORINTHIANS 15:58

Standing for what's right will always meet opposition from those who don't love God.

We know the world opposed Jesus, so why wouldn't the world also oppose those who follow Him? Jesus warned us about this:

"If you belonged to the world, the world would love you as its
own. You do not belong to the world. I have chosen
you out of the world and the world hates you."

JOHN 15:19

Remember Noah? Bible scholars believe he spent decades—between fifty-five and seventy-five years—faithfully building the ark. We know the people around him were wicked, and we can imagine that they mocked him. They probably whispered that Noah was crazy. Who would build a giant boat in the middle of dry land?

No doubt it would have been easier for Noah to quit building the ark, but God had told him to do it, so Noah stood firm.

He was six hundred years old when the flood finally came. Here's what happened to the wicked people around him:

All flesh that moved on the earth was destroyed,
birds and cattle and wild animals, and every man.

GENESIS 7:21

Misplaced confidence can be deadly. Jesus said the people of Noah's day kept doing what they'd always done—eating, drinking, starting families—right up to the day Noah entered the ark (Luke 17:27). But they were confident about the wrong things, since Jesus said, "the flood came and killed all the people on earth."

What should give us confidence is the Gospel. Thinking of Jesus and what He's done for us will help us to stand firm. In fact, if we're ever tempted to quit, the Bible tells us to remember what Jesus experienced for us.

> *Sinful men spoke words of hate against Christ.*
> *He was willing to take such shame from sinners.*
> *Think of this so you will not get tired and give up.*
> HEBREWS 12:3

Whether you can stand firm and hold fast to your faith is largely determined by your answer to one important question: Where do you look for your daily encouragement?

If your answer is anything other than God and His Word, you are setting yourself up for failure. God is the only sustaining power in the universe. No human being can be trusted the way God can.

He will help you stand firm. Not only is He able, but He is willing.

¡ASPIRE TO KNOW MORE

▶ Read Matthew 24:37-44. According to these verses, how is Noah's story similar to what will happen when Jesus returns?

▶ Hebrews 11 is called the "Hall of Faith" chapter because it lists men and women who were heroes in the Bible. The people in the Bible aren't just story characters—they're real people who lived on our planet. How is Noah described in verse 7?

97

¡ASPIRE TO BE AN EXAMPLE

Let no one show little respect for you because you are young.
Show other Christians how to live by your life. They should be
able to follow you in the way you talk and in what you do.
Show them how to live in faith and in love and in holy living.

1 TIMOTHY 4:12

Everything you do matters. *Everything.*

Every decision you make either points people toward or away from Christ. You represent Jesus.

Everyone who knows you are a Christian (which should be a lot of people, since you shouldn't keep this news a secret) is watching to see the way you live. Your decisions, actions, and reactions have the power to make people think good things or bad things about God. As Jesus said,

"Let your light shine in front of men. Then they
will see the good things you do and will
honor your Father Who is in heaven."

MATTHEW 5:16

Light in this verse is another word for testimony or example. God wants you to make good choices to please Him, but your good decisions can also point a watching world to a waiting Savior.

First Corinthians is a letter the apostle Paul wrote to believers in the area of Corinth, Greece. He told them, "Follow my example, as I follow the example of Christ" (1 Corinthians 11:1 NIV). Can you imagine living so confidently for the glory of God that you could say to other people, "Follow my example"? This is God's desire for your life. In fact, He wants you to have an eternal impact.

You may be thinking, *Being an example is a lot of pressure. I make mistakes! There's no way I can be perfect.* And you're right. Nobody besides Jesus ever walked or will walk perfectly on this earth. Thankfully, we don't have to live perfectly to be a good example.

When we inevitably mess up, we can still honor God by the way we respond. Humbly asking forgiveness of others is a powerful example of real Christianity.

You may be thinking, *I'm too young to be an example. I'm still following the example of others!* And you should be watching the example of godly people. You may find them in your home, at church, or in Christian biographies—read the stories of people like George Müller, C. S. Lewis, Elisabeth Elliot, or Corrie ten Boom.

But you're never too young to be an example. Even younger kids are looking up to you right now. And people who don't know Jesus are very curious about your life and the choices you make.

What do they see when they watch your life? Let it be someone who loves God and makes decisions to please Him.

¡ASPIRE TO KNOW MORE

▶ Find Psalm 71:5. Is this something you can pray to God?

▶ Think of the people you know and love. Whose example can you follow? To whom can you be an example?

98

¡ASPIRE TO KEEP GOING

Do not let yourselves get tired of doing good. If we do not
give up, we will get what is coming to us at the right time.
GALATIANS 6:9

We've all experienced a setback at one time or another. A setback is something that stops you from making progress or moving forward on your goals. Maybe your goal is to make an A in a class, but you fail a quiz. Or maybe you're trying to control your temper, but on a bad day you blow up at somebody. Life is filled with setbacks, both small and large.

Does God care about our setbacks? Of course. He cares about everything in our lives. Perhaps the bigger question is "What does He expect from us in these moments?"

Here's what the apostle Paul said:

This is the reason we do not give up. Our human
body is wearing out. But our spirits are getting stronger
every day. The little troubles we suffer now for a short
time are making us ready for the great things God is
going to give us forever. We do not look at the things that
can be seen. We look at the things that cannot be seen.
The things that can be seen will come to an end. But
the things that cannot be seen will last forever.
2 CORINTHIANS 4:16–18

Very simply, when you make mistakes or face reverses, don't let those setbacks become campsites. In other words, keep going. Don't stay there. Don't come back and revisit your losses.

If you've sinned, admit it and ask forgiveness. *Then move on.*

In the Bible, we read about a man named Saul. In his own words, he "persecuted the church of God violently and tried to destroy it" (Galatians 1:13 ESV). He became famous for hurting and killing people who worshipped God. But then something incredible happened: one day on the road to Damascus—where Saul was traveling to harm more Christians—God stopped him and *saved* him. And Saul became Paul, who did big things for God and wrote much of the New Testament. An amazing missionary who took the Gospel to people all over the world, Paul's writing still impacts people for the glory of God.

When Paul was Saul, he made really bad choices. But he chose to accept God's forgiveness and move on to better things. What might have happened if Paul kept thinking about his mistakes and all the harm he had done? What if he'd allowed his evil past to paralyze him from moving on and serving God? Would he have been as useful in ministry?

Whether your past is filled with shameful mistakes, private sins, or pesky setbacks, the solution is the same: ask God to forgive you when you fail and then *keep going.*

Aspire to keep going, especially when times are tough.

¡ASPIRE TO KNOW MORE

- ▶ Find 1 Timothy 1:12–17. What does Paul have to say about the wrong choices he made? Did they ruin his life or did God use them for good?

- ▶ Read 1 John 4:18. Does God want us to be afraid of making mistakes?

99

¡ASPIRE TO BE FAITHFUL

*"He that is faithful with little things is faithful
with big things also. He that is not honest with
little things is not honest with big things."*

Do you want to do big and important things when you're an adult?

If so, great! Start *today* by being faithful with your smaller responsibilities and opportunities. Homework, chores, practicing, and work may not seem big or exciting, but these are the tasks God has given to you today, and He wants you to be faithful in them. When you're faithful in your work, you're actually being faithful to God.

You can aspire to be faithful to God because He has already promised to be faithful to you:

*"Know then that the Lord your God is God,
the faithful God. He keeps His promise and shows
His loving-kindness to those who love Him and keep
His Laws, even to a thousand family groups in the future."*

DEUTERONOMY 7:9

The good news: trusting God to be faithful to you requires no real risk on your part.

It's like when you and your friend dare each other to do something, and your friend counts down—*3, 2, 1*—and you hesitate ever so slightly because you want to make sure he or she actually follows through before you act. You don't want to be the only one looking dumb or eating something gross or doing something silly.

When it comes to God's faithfulness, you don't ever have to wonder if

He won't follow through or keep His end of the promise. The countdown has already happened. History has already been written. God has already proven that He will be faithful to His Word every single time.

If you are a child of God, you have no reason to doubt that immediately after your last breath on earth, you'll take your next breath in the presence of your Creator. And you'll recognize that He has been unshakably faithful to you through your entire life—just like He was faithful to hundreds of generations ahead of you.

The only real question is whether *you* will be faithful to *Him*.

It may cost you something. You may lose friends or opportunities along the way. You may get laughed at or rejected. You may even be persecuted for your faith.

But no matter what happens in this life, faithfulness to God is always worth it.

Aspire to be faithful to God no matter what. He'll make it worth every sacrifice.

¡ASPIRE TO KNOW MORE

- ▶ Find the word *faithful* in a dictionary. What does it mean to be faithful?

- ▶ Look up Hebrews 13:8. What does this verse have to do with faithfulness?

- ▶ Write 1 Thessalonians 5:24 on a note card and put it somewhere you'll see it when you need to be encouraged.

100

¡ASPIRE TO KEEP GOD FIRST

Even more than that, I think of everything as worth nothing.
It is so much better to know Christ Jesus my Lord. I have
lost everything for Him. And I think of these things as
worth nothing so that I can have Christ.

PHILIPPIANS 3:8

Right now in your life, lots of things feel important. You may have goals you want to accomplish, things you want to learn, people you want to meet. You may hope to get married someday, or maybe you plan to have kids. Additionally, school is important, church is important, and family is important.

There's nothing wrong with having hope for the future. Goals and dreams are great, but remember, they aren't everything.

At the end of the day—and at the end of your *life*—the only thing that will matter is your relationship with God. Did you love Him? Did you obey Him? Did you really *know* Him?

Here's the secret to living your best life: seek God with all your heart. That's it: just keep God first.

In Matthew 22, a group of proud religious leaders decided to trap Jesus by asking Him which of the laws was the greatest. In other words, they wanted Jesus to tell them which of the hundreds of Old Testament commandments was the most important one. No doubt they planned to use Jesus' answer against Him.

But instead of talking about what people should eat or wear or say, Jesus said something unexpected:

> " 'You must love the Lord your God with all your heart
> and with all your soul and with all your mind.'
> This is the first and greatest of the Laws."

MATTHEW 22:37–38

It was true for the people Jesus taught, and it's true for you today. The greatest choice you can make with your life is to love God and keep Him first.

In fact, if there is only one thing you take away from this book, let it be this: *keep God first*. And you know how to do that? By loving God most.

God has never faced anything that was too hard. He can be nothing other than good. He is true to His Word, and if you are a believer in Jesus, He has redeemed your soul. Never get over that.

God wants to be your first priority—the first person you come to with good or bad news. He wants you to pray to Him, talk to Him, sing to Him, live for Him. And He'll help you do it.

Love God more than you love your life, and you will live to the fullest.

¡ASPIRE TO KNOW MORE

- ▶ Find Romans 8:28. Christians love this verse (and they should!), but for whom does the Bible say all things will work together for good?

- ▶ Read Psalm 63:1-2, a good picture of loving God most. Is this how you feel? If not, stop and ask God to help you love Him more. (He'll do it!)

101

¡ASPIRE TO FINISH WELL

*All these many people who have had faith in God are
around us like a cloud. Let us put every thing out of our
lives that keeps us from doing what we should. Let us keep
running in the race that God has planned for us.*

HEBREWS 12:1

Run your own race. Don't worry about the race other people are running. Don't waste your time wishing you could run a different, better track. God has called you to live at a specific time in a specific place for a specific purpose. The fact that you are living on this earth right now is by divine design.

No one else can live the life God has intentionally called *you* to live. So run your race for the glory of God. Say with the apostle Paul,

*I do one thing. I forget everything that is behind me and look
forward to that which is ahead of me. My eyes are on the
crown. I want to win the race and get the crown
of God's call from heaven through Christ Jesus.*

PHILIPPIANS 3:13–14

In any race—but especially in the race of life—it is much harder to end well than it is to begin well. But it is always more important how the race concludes.

So how do we run in order to finish *life* well? Here are four key ideas: (1) spend time with God every day; (2) share the Gospel every chance you get; (3) commit to serve God with your life no matter what happens; (4) trust God completely.

If you're thinking you can't do these things on your own, you're right.

Left to ourselves, we can achieve nothing good. But being preoccupied with our limitations is self-centered and unhelpful. Our motivation for everything we do must be *Jesus*. He died for you, rose again, and now wants to help you live in a way that pleases Him.

So be single-minded, keeping your eyes fixed on Christ, and you'll be just fine.

The words that the apostle Paul left with the Thessalonians are appropriate to leave you with as well:

> *Our Lord Jesus Christ and God our Father loves us.*
> *Through His loving-favor He gives us comfort and hope*
> *that lasts forever. May He give your hearts comfort*
> *and strength to say and do every good thing.*
> 2 THESSALONIANS 2:16–17

Now go. . .aspire to *live* your life for the glory of God.

¡ASPIRE TO KNOW MORE

▶ On a piece of paper, write out where you'd like to be with God in one, five, and ten years. Then put that paper in a place where you'll see it regularly.

▶ Find John 17:4. These are the words Jesus prayed shortly before He would die on the cross for humanity's sins. These are words we should each aspire to say at the end of our lives.

▶ Read Philippians 1:6. What confidence do we have that we can finish living this life to the glory of God?